On June 27, 2008, my life was perfect. On June 28, 2008, my life was blown away when my youngest son was falsely accused of felony murder. False witnesses were rising up daily, and there was no way out. The best attorney in the Southeast gave us very little hope—the lies were stacked too high against my son. After trying for six months to fix it myself, I found myself in a hospital bed dying of exhaustion and a broken heart. When I was released from the hospital, I went by CVS to get my medication, and my eyes were drawn to the Choice book rack where I saw the book *Psalm 91: God's Shield of Protection* by Peggy Joyce Ruth.

I took it home, climbed into my prayer closet, and started reading about miracle after miracle where God had intervened in impossible situations and did the supernatural. I had to have one of those miracles! I moved my life into the Book of Psalms and started claiming Psalm 91 for our family's miracle.

My son did indeed end up being tried for murder, with no hope outside of our miracle through Psalm 91. God was all we had, but God was all we needed as He showed up on April 16, 2009, and moved our mountain with His supernatural power. Afterward I wrote two books that have now been filmed as *A Cry for Justice*—all because of Psalm 91 and the power it holds within, just waiting for our claiming. Thank you, Peggy Joyce Ruth, for introducing me to our Deliverer!

Psalm 91 for Mothers is a book that will help all mothers make it through another day in times of trouble and trials.

—Jackie Carpenter

Author of *The Bridge: Between "Cell Block A" and a "Miracle" Is Psalm 91* and *Georgia Justice*

Executive Producer, *A Cry for Justice*

PSALM 91 for MOTHERS

PEGGY JOYCE RUTH

ANGELIA RUTH SCHUM

Most Charisma House Book Group products are available at special quantity discounts for bulk purchase for sales promotions, premiums, fund-raising, and educational needs. For details, write Charisma House Book Group, 600 Rinehart Road, Lake Mary, Florida 32746, or telephone (407) 333-0600.

Psalm 91 for Mothers by Peggy Joyce Ruth
and Angelia Ruth Schum
Published by Charisma House
Charisma Media/Charisma House Book Group
600 Rinehart Road
Lake Mary, Florida 32746
www.charismahouse.com

Cover design by Justin Evans
Design Director: Bill Johnson

Visit the author's website at www.peggyjoyceruth.org.

Library of Congress Cataloging-in-Publication Data:

Ruth, Peggy Joyce.
Psalm 91 for mothers / Peggy Joyce Ruth, Angelia Ruth Schum.
pages cm
Includes bibliographical references (pages).
ISBN 978-1-61638-734-1 (trade paper) -- ISBN 978-1-61638-735-8 (ebook)
1. Bible. O.T. Psalms XCI--Meditations. 2. Mothers--Religious life. I. Schum, Angelia Ruth. II. Title.

BS145091st .R88 2013
223'.206--dc23

2012043109

Portions of this book were previously published by Charisma House in *Psalm 91*, copyright © 2010, ISBN 978-1-61638-147-9.

While the author has made every effort to provide accurate telephone numbers and Internet addresses at the time of publication, neither the publisher nor the author assumes any responsibility for errors or for changes that occur after publication.

20 21 22 23 24 — 13 12 11 10 9
Printed in the United States of America

CONTENTS

Preface: Setting the Scene ix

Introduction: Those Days When You Need Psalm 91 xiii

1 Where Is My Dwelling Place? 1

2 What Is Coming Out of My Mouth? 9

3 Two-Way Deliverance 17

4 Under His Wings 23

5 A Mighty Fortress Is My God 27

6 I Will Not Fear the Terror 33

7 I Will Not Fear the Arrow 41

8 I Will Not Be Afraid of the Pestilence 47

9 I Will Not Fear the Destruction 51

10 Though a Thousand Fall 57

11 No Plague Comes Near My Family 65

12 Angels Are Watching Over Me 75

13 The Enemy Is Under My Feet 83

14 Because I Love Him 95

15 God Is My Deliverer 101

16 I Am Seated on High 109

17 God Answers My Call 115

18 God Rescues Me From Trouble 119

19 God Honors Me 127

20 God Satisfies Me With Long Life 131

21 I Behold His Salvation 141

Summary 151

What Must I Do to Be Saved? 153

Prayer Covenant 157

Notes 159

Preface

SETTING the SCENE

SUNDAYS WERE USUALLY A comfort—but not on this particular Sunday! Our pastor looked unusually serious that day as he made the announcement that one of our most beloved and faithful deacons had been diagnosed with leukemia and had only a few weeks to live. Only the Sunday before, this robust-looking deacon in his mid-forties had been in his regular place in the choir, looking as healthy and happy as ever. Now, one Sunday later, the entire congregation was in a state of shock after hearing such an unexpected announcement. However, little did I know this incident would pave the way to a message that was going to forever burn in my heart.

Surprisingly I had gone home from church that day feeling very little fear, perhaps because I was numb from the shock of what I had heard. I vividly remember sitting down on the edge of the bed that afternoon and saying out loud: "Lord, we have two young children. Is there any way for our family to be protected from all the evils that are coming on the earth?" I was not expecting an answer; I was merely voicing the thought that kept replaying over and over in my mind. I remember lying across the bed and falling immediately to sleep, only to wake up a short five minutes later. However, in those five minutes I had a very unusual dream.

In the dream I was in an open field, asking the same question that I had prayed earlier—"Is there any way to be protected from all the things that are coming on the earth?" And in my dream, I heard these words:

> In your day of trouble call upon Me, and I will answer you!

Suddenly I knew I had the answer I had so long been searching for. The ecstatic joy I felt was beyond anything I could ever describe. To my surprise, instantly there were hundreds with me in the dream out in that open field, praising and thanking God for the answer. It wasn't until the next day, however, when I heard the Ninety-First Psalm referred to on a tape by Shirley Boone, that I suddenly *knew in my heart* that *whatever* was in that psalm was God's answer to my question. I nearly tore up my Bible in my haste to see what it said. There it was in verse 15—the *exact statement* God had spoken to me in my dream. I could hardly believe my eyes!

I believe that you who are reading this book, and especially those of you with children for whom you are concerned, are among the many Christians to whom God is supernaturally revealing this psalm. You were the ones pictured with me in my dream in that open field who will, through the message in this book, get your answer to the question, "Can a Christian be protected through these turbulent times?"

Since the early 1970s I have had many opportunities to share this message. I feel God has commissioned me to write this book to proclaim God's *covenant of protection*. May you be sincerely blessed by it.

—Peggy Joyce Ruth

Introduction

THOSE DAYS WHEN YOU NEED PSALM 91

SOMETIMES YOU FORGET YOUR purse, your cell phone, your briefcase, your cup of coffee...that had been temporarily perched on the top of the car when you anxiously jumped in the driver's seat and took off in a flash to avoid being late for your next appointment. How frustrating to later realize you left your cell phone on top of the car—and experience the sickening feeling of how expensive a stupid mistake like that can be. You recall the subconscious anxiety that grips you when you know you have to face your husband and explain what happened to your new cell phone!

But nothing could be as bad as what Donna Newsom saw that morning in Dallas traffic. With horror she realized *what* was perched on top of the car in front of her. She recalls that experience below.

> Rush hour traffic in the Dallas Metropolis was not for the faint of heart. Heat rose from the pavement in waves as I nosed my white Mustang out of the Winn-Dixie parking lot and into the maze of cars and trucks headed home.
>
> Traffic at a crawl, I hummed the notes of a song I'd sung at Fox Avenue Baptist Church. The words, like the message behind them, had lingered in my mind for days. "*Hide me in the shadow of Your wings*..."
>
> I knew that the words referred to Psalm 91. The first verse began, "He that dwelleth in the secret place of the most High shall abide under the shadow of the Almighty" (KJV). Verse 4 says, "He shall cover thee with his feathers, and under his wings shalt thou trust" (KJV). I'd heard stories for years about soldiers who'd survived horrifying situations by praying and believing that psalm.
>
> The message had become more personal when I attended a conference and heard a more in-depth teaching on Psalm 91's promise of divine protection. Since then I'd come face-to-face with numerous

situations that should have ended in tragedy. In each case I'd witnessed supernatural protection.

It had happened enough that I wondered if God might be trying to tell me something.

"Pay attention! This is real!"

As a registered nurse I'd witnessed so much death and tragedy that perhaps I'd stopped expecting to see miracles right before my eyes. Had I forgotten that God never changes? That His promises are as true today as when He spoke them? Had I put more faith in the medical profession than in God's Word?

Nudging my way through traffic, I eased into the turn lane behind a dark blue station wagon. The light turned, and, looking up, I froze at the sight before me.

On top of the blue car was an infant seat. Surely it was empty! No, *heaven have mercy*, there was a baby in it. Without having a moment to attempt to process this horror scene, I screamed the name that is above all names, *"Jesus!"*

Just as I did, the station wagon accelerated into a left turn. And in the space of a heartbeat the infant seat slid across the roof of the car.

"Jesus!"

Airborne now, the baby was catapulted through the air like a tossed egg. Horns honked and brakes squealed as, like me, other drivers watched in a slow-motion nightmare as the car turned east and the baby was jet-propelled north—straight into traffic.

"Jesus!"

The infant seat hit the pavement and bounced before skidding to a stop.

Slamming on my brakes, I swerved, missing the baby. I flew out of my car at a dead run as other cars squealed to a stop. Heart hammering in my chest, my hands shook as I dropped in the street.

The carrier had landed right side up. Dressed in pink, her fat little legs churning, the baby grinned at me as drool dribbled down her chin. That's when I heard the screams.

"My baby! My baby! My baby!"

Tears streamed from bruised eyes hollow from lack of sleep. I glanced at her car, still idling in the intersection. The wide-eyed faces of several small children stared back at me.

I turned to a bystander. "Get that car off the street! And watch those kids!"

I spoke to the mother with calm authority. "I'm a nurse," I said. "Come on, let's get her out of the street, and then I'll check her for injuries."

On the shoulder of the road I checked the baby from head to toe. There wasn't a single scratch on her. I knelt there for a heartbeat, watching the baby smile.

"It's OK," I told the mother. "She isn't hurt."

The woman fell into my arms, sobbing with relief. "Thank you," she hiccupped through her tears. "I can't thank you enough."

Moments later an ambulance and a police car screamed to the scene. They transported the baby to Lewisville Memorial Hospital, where I worked, and asked me to go along. The emergency room doctor did a more thorough exam. "There's not a scratch on her," he said, shaking his head in awe.

The mother had set the infant, buckled in her carrier, on top of the car while she put the other children in their seat belts. Then, running on the fumes of sleep-deprived exhaustion, she'd climbed into the car and driven off.

What were the chances that a baby would survive being hurled into traffic? That the infant seat would land right side up and skid to a complete stop just like a plane landing on a runway? Those cars had scattered in time, and none of them hit the baby. There wasn't a single wreck, no multiple car pileups—not even a fender bender.

Climbing back into my Mustang, I rested my forehead on the steering wheel. I knew the answer. That child had been hidden in the shadow of His wing.

Pulling back in traffic, I headed home singing a love song to Jesus. "Hide me in the shadow of Your wings..."

Message received, Lord. Loud and clear.

You know the fear you sometimes feel when you are traveling behind a reckless motorcycle driver—knowing if he falls over, it will be next to impossible to avoid hitting him. You can imagine the tension Donna felt traveling behind a car with a baby on top!

God has offered for Psalm 91 to be in your life *for days like this*!

Chapter

WHERE IS MY DWELLING PLACE?

> He who dwells in the shelter of the Most High will abide in the shadow of the Almighty.
>
> —Psalm 91:1

Think for just a minute of where, more than anyplace else in the world, you like to be when you want to feel protected and peaceful. I remember when I was a little girl and would wake up in the middle of the night and feel frightened. I would tiptoe down to my mother and dad's room and very quietly slip in bed with them. As I lay there—silently listening to them breathe and feeling all cozy and protected—before I knew it, the fear was gone, and I would be sound asleep.

I am sure you can think of something that represents *security* to you personally. When I think of security and protection, I have a couple of childhood memories that automatically come to mind. My dad was a large, muscular man who played football during his high school and college years, but he interrupted his education to serve in the military during World War II. Mother, who was pregnant with my little brother, and I lived with my grandparents in San Saba while Dad was in the service. As young as I was, I vividly remember one ecstatically happy day when my dad unexpectedly opened the door and walked into my grandmother's living room. Before that eventful day I had been tormented with fears because some neighborhood children had told me I would never see my dad again. Like kids telling a ghost story, they taunted me that my dad would come home in a box. When he walked through that door that day, *a sense of peace and security came over me and stayed with me for the rest of his time in the army.*

My father, Albert Crow

It was past time for my baby brother to be born, and I found out when I was older that Dad's outfit at the time was being relocated by train from Long Beach, California, to Virginia Beach, Virginia. The train was coming through Fort Worth, Texas, on its way to Virginia, so my dad caught a ride from Fort Worth to San Saba in the hopes of seeing his new son. He then hitchhiked until he caught up with the train shortly before it reached Virginia Beach. The memory of his walking into that room still brings a feeling of peaceful calm to my soul. In fact, that incident set the stage for later seeking the security a *heavenly* Father's presence could bring.

When I think of dwelling in the shelter of God, I have another childhood memory that always comes to mind. My parents would often take my younger brother and sister and me to a lake. There was a wonderful place to fish for perch that very few people knew about, and we children loved to perch fish. It was such a thrill to see the cork begin to bobble and then suddenly go completely out of sight. There were very few things that I liked better than jerking back on that old cane pole and landing a huge perch. Dad had a good reason for having us catch those perch. They were what he used for bait on the trotline that he

Dad and family on fishing trip

had stretched out across one of the secret coves at the lake.

Dad would drive the boat over to the place where his trotline was located. Then he would cut off the boat motor and inch the boat across the water as he *ran the trotline*. That's what he called it when he would hold onto to the trotline with his hands and pull the boat alongside all the hooks he had baited in hopes that he had caught a big catfish. A trotline was like having about twenty-five fishing poles baited and placed all the way across the lake.

I loved to perch fish, but it was an even greater thrill when Dad would get to a place where the trotline rope would begin to jerk almost out of his hand. That meant he had hooked a fish. It was then that all three of us children would watch, wide-eyed, as Dad wrestled with that line until finally, in victory, he would flip that huge catfish over the side of the boat, right at our feet. Money could never buy that kind of excitement! The circus and a carnival all rolled up into one couldn't give us that kind of a thrill.

One of those outings proved to be more exciting than most, turning out to be an action-packed experience that I will never forget. It had been a beautiful day when we started out, but by the time we finished our perch fishing and were headed toward the trotline, everything changed. A storm came up on the lake so suddenly there was no time to get back to the boat dock. The sky turned black, lightning was flashing, and drops of rain were falling so hard that they stung our skin when they hit. Then, moments later, we were in the middle of a hailstorm with large, marble-sized hail.

I could see the fear in my mother's eyes, and I knew we were in danger. But before I had time to wonder what we were going to do, Dad had driven the boat to the rugged shoreline of the only island on the lake. There are many boat docks that surround the island now, but back then it looked like an abandoned island with absolutely no place to take refuge from the storm. In just moments Dad had us all out of the boat and ordered the three of us to lie down beside our mother on the ground. Quickly pulling a canvas tarp out of the bottom of the boat, he knelt down on the ground beside us and pulled that tarp up over all five of us. That storm raged outside the homemade tent he had made—the rain beat down, the lightning flashed, and the thunder rolled. But all I could think about was how it felt to have his arms around us. There was a certain peace that is hard to explain as we lay there under the protection of the shield my father had provided. In fact, I had never felt as safe and secure in my entire life. I can remember thinking that I wished the storm would last forever. I didn't want anything to spoil the wonderful security I felt that day—there *in our secret hiding place.* Feeling my father's strong, protective arms around me, I wanted it to never end.

Although I have never forgotten that experience when we were fishing at the lake, today it has taken on new meaning. Just as Dad put a tarp over us to shield us from the storm, our heavenly Father has a *secret place* in His arms that protects us from the storms that are raging in the world around us.

Fear is running rampant in the world today. Even children who have the security of a home filled with the love of a mother and father cannot help but sense the growing anxiety that is plaguing our schools, our streets, our newspapers, and our televisions. Suicides are becoming a common occurrence. But did you know that this place in God is real for anyone who wants to seek refuge in Him? *It is a literal place of physical safety and security that God tells us about in this Psalm 91.*

This *secret place* is literal, but it is also conditional! In verse 1 of Psalm 91 God lists our part of the condition before He even mentions the promises included in His part. That's because *our part* has to come first. To abide in the *shadow* of the Almighty, we must first *choose to dwell* in the shelter of the Most High.

The question is, how do we dwell in the security and shelter of the Most High? It is more than an intellectual experience. This verse speaks of a dwelling place in which we can be physically protected if we run to Him. You may utterly believe that God is your refuge, and you may give mental assent to it in your prayer time, but unless you *actually get up and run to the shelter*—you will never experience it. I call that place of refuge a *love walk*!

Most children have a secret hideout where they feel all safe and secure, hidden away from the whole world. They need to be taught, however, that those places where they feel protected are nice, but a hideout cannot keep them safe from everything. It will be life changing, however, when they are told that there is a place of shelter that will keep them protected from every evil this world has ever known. What a treasure you are leaving them when you teach them that God says He is a place of real safety from any bad thing they can think of in the whole earth—if they will run to Him. And how do they run to God? They don't run there with their feet. They run to God with their heart! They need to be taught that they are running to God every time they think about Him—every time they tell the Lord that they love Him.

Cullen and Meritt

When our grandchildren Cullen and Meritt were young, they would often stay the night with us. The moment they finished breakfast, each would run to his own secret place to spend some time talking with God. Cullen found a place behind the couch in the den, and Meritt headed behind the lamp table in the corner of our bedroom. Those places became very special to them.

Where is your secret place? Everyone needs the security and shelter of a secret place with the Most High.

Chapter

WHAT IS COMING OUT of MY MOUTH?

I will say to the LORD, "My refuge and my fortress, my God, in whom I trust!"

—PSALM 91:2

DID YOU NOTICE THAT God says that you are supposed to *say out loud* that *God* is your *place of safety and protection*? He wants you to tell Him that you trust Him. It is not enough to just think about God. When you say God's Word out loud and believe it—something happens in the spiritual realm.

It is easy to see why God likes for us to say it out loud to Him. How would someone feel if he lived in the house with his mother and father and saw them every day, but they never said anything out loud to him? That wouldn't feel very good, would it? When you tell God that you believe Him when He says He will protect you—God hears it, His angels hear it, and the devil also hears it. Then God can say, "Devil, you cannot hurt him. He believes My Word, and he is protected," and God's angels go to work to protect you as well.

So many times we are doing everything we can think of to protect ourselves, and, to a point, that is not bad. It is good to eat healthy food and obey safety rules and even go to a doctor when we need to. God is pleased when we do things that are wise, but those things cannot always protect us. God is the only one who can protect us from *whatever* the problem might be.

Do you know why God calls us His *sheep*? It's because a sheep is the only animal that doesn't have any protection on its own. It is not like a dog that can bark away his enemies or a skunk that can spray out a bad odor to keep from being bothered. Some animals have sharp teeth to protect themselves, but a sheep doesn't have anything to protect himself—*except the shepherd*. We are God's sheep, and Jesus is our good Shepherd. He wants us to know that He is our protector. Just as the shepherds on the hillside protect their sheep, Jesus wants to protect us.

When I get afraid that something bad is going to happen, I say out loud, "Jesus, You are my Shepherd, and I am Your sheep. I know You will protect me because You promised that in Psalm 91, so I am not going to fear. In Jesus' name I tell that fear to leave me now."

Another time when God brought life to a death situation stands out in my mind. The whole family was rejoicing when our daughter-in-law, Sloan, received a positive pregnancy test report and found she was going to have the first grandchild on either side of the family. Since she'd had a tubal pregnancy once before, making her highly susceptible for another, the doctor ordered a sonogram as a precautionary measure.

The disturbing result of the sonogram was: "no fetus found, a great deal of water in the uterus and spots of endometriosis." With only two hours' notice, emergency surgery was quickly underway, at which time the doctor performed a laparoscopy, drained the uterus, and scraped away the endometriosis. After the surgery the doctor's words were, "During the laparoscopy we carefully looked everywhere, and there was no sign of a baby, but I want to see you back in my office in one week to be sure fluid doesn't build back up." When Sloan argued that the pregnancy test had been positive, he said there was a 99 percent chance the baby had naturally aborted and had been absorbed into the uterine lining.

Even so, after the doctor left the room, Sloan was the only one not fazed by his report. What she said next surprised everyone. She emphatically stated that even the doctor had left her with a 1 percent chance, and she was going to take it. From that moment on no amount of discouragement from well-meaning friends who didn't want her to be disappointed had any effect on her. Never once did she veer away from confessing out loud Psalm 91 and another Scripture promise that she had found: "[My child] will not die, but live, and tell of the works of the LORD" (Ps. 118:17).

A strange look came on the technician's face the next week as she administered the ultrasound. She immediately called for the physician. Her reaction was a little disconcerting to Sloan until Sloan heard these words: "Doctor, I think you need to come here quickly. I've just found a six-week-old fetus!" It was nothing short of a miracle that such severe, invasive procedures had not damaged or destroyed this delicate life in its beginning stages. When I

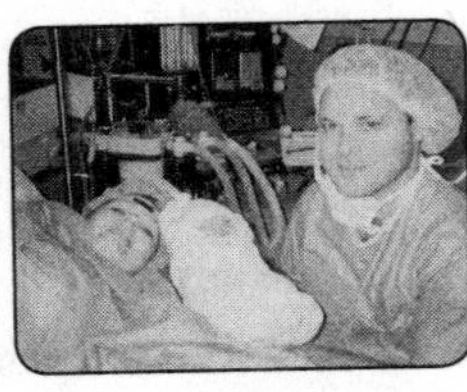

Proud daddy Bill holding newborn Cullen

look at my grandson, it is hard to imagine life without him. I thank God for a daughter-in-law who believes in her covenant and is not ashamed *to confess it out loud* in the face of every negative report.

God wants you to believe His Word more than you believe some person who is telling you something different—no matter how smart and important you think that individual is. God is faithful to His Word if we trust Him.

Notice that verse 2 at the beginning of Psalm 91 says, "I will say..." Circle the word *say* in your Bible, because we must learn to verbalize our trust. No place in the Bible does it tell us to *think* the Word. There is something about *saying* it that releases power in the spiritual realm. We are told to meditate on the Word—but when you look up that word *meditate*, it means "to mutter." We answer back to God what He says to us in the first verse. There is power in saying His Word back to Him!

Joel 3:10 tells the weak to say, "I am a mighty man." Over and over we find great men of God like David, Joshua, Shadrach, Meshach, and Abednego declaring their confessions of faith aloud in dangerous situations. Notice what begins to happen on the inside when you say, "Lord, You are my refuge... You are my fortress... You are my Lord and my God! It is in You that I put my total trust!" The more we say it aloud, the more confident we become in His protection.

So many times as Christians we mentally agree that the Lord is our refuge—but that is not enough. Power is released in saying it out loud. When we say it and mean it, we are placing ourselves in His shelter. By voicing His Lordship and His protection, we open the door to the secret place.

Have you ever tried to protect yourself from all the bad things that can happen? God knows we can't do it. Psalm 60:11 tells us, "...deliverance by man is in vain." God has to be our refuge before the promises in Psalm 91 will ever work.

Some quote Psalm 91 as though it were some kind of "magic wand," but there is nothing magical about this psalm. It is powerful, and it works simply because it is the Word of God, alive and active. And we confess it aloud simply because the Bible tells us to do so.

Did you know that God has given you the *name of Jesus* and the *Holy Scriptures* to speak and use as weapons to fight the enemy and evil spirits that can work through evil people? But those weapons will do us no good if we don't know how to use them. Most everyone knows how to use a physical weapon. If I handed you a gun or a knife, you would not try to use your foot and your big toe to make it work. Of course not! You know to use your hand and fingers to operate physical weapons. But most people do not know what part of the body to use to make spiritual weapons work. *You operate spiritual weapons with your mouth and your tongue.* Every word you speak is a spiritual weapon—either for good or for evil.

Did you know that your words are very powerful? Every word you speak with faith will change things for good or for bad. That is why it is so important to say what God's Word says. If you say negative things that go against God's Word, you bring negative, evil things into your life. For example, when you say things like, "I'm always sick," or "I hate my brother [or sister]," or "I don't want to read God's Word," or "God let me down," you are using Satan's weapons. What comes out of your mouth is firing either God's weapon or Satan's weapon.

> Death and life are in the power of the tongue.
>
> —Proverbs 18:21

When I'm facing a challenge, I have learned to say, "In this particular situation ____________________ [name the situation aloud] I choose to trust You, Lord." The difference it makes when I proclaim my trust aloud is amazing.

Take notice of what flies out of your mouth in times of trouble. The worst thing that can happen is for something to come out that brings death. Cursing gives God nothing to work with. This psalm tells us to do just the opposite—speak life!

Our part of this protection covenant is expressed in verses 1 and 2 of Psalm 91. Note very carefully these words: "he who *dwells*..." and "I will *say*..." These words, which amount to *our responsibility* under the terms of this covenant, release God's power to fulfill His amazing promises given to us in verses 3 through 16.

Chapter

TWO-WAY DELIVERANCE

> For it is He who delivers you from the snare of the trapper and from the deadly pestilence.
>
> —Psalm 91:3

Have you ever seen a movie where a fur trapper travels deep into the mountains in the cold climate? He baits big, steel traps, covers them over with branches, and then waits for some unsuspecting animal to step into the trap. Those traps were not there by chance. The trapper has taken great care in placing them in very strategic locations. In times of war a minefield is set up the same way. Those land mines are methodically placed in well-calculated locations.

These are pictures of what the enemy does to us. That is why he is called the *trapper*! The traps that are set for us are not there by accident. It is as if the trap has your name on it. They are custom made, placed, and baited specifically for each one of us. But like an animal caught in a trap, when ensnared, we suffer through a slow, painful process. We don't die instantly. We are ensnared until the trapper comes to destroy us.

Our children need to be taught that Satan's main trick is to tempt them to sin. That temptation is one of Satan's traps. If they fall for the temptation, and sin, it is like getting caught in the trap, and bad things happen.

The enemy knows exactly what will most likely hook us, and he knows exactly which thought to put into our minds to lure us into the trap. That is why Paul tells us in 2 Corinthians 2:11 that we are "not [to be] ignorant of his schemes." Then he says:

> For the weapons of our warfare are not of the flesh, but divinely powerful for the destruction of fortresses. We are destroying speculations and every lofty thing raised up against the knowledge

of God, and we are taking every thought captive to the obedience of Christ.

—2 Corinthians 10:4–5

Sometimes the traps of the enemy are *physical* traps sent to destroy you. In the town where we live there is a sulfur spring, and when we were young, it was a swimming pool filled with sulfur water. My dad had a back injury, and the doctor wanted him to float in that warm sulfur water every day. We loved the idea because Dad bought season swimming passes for all of us, and the moment he got home from work, we would all head for the pool to swim while Dad floated.

My brother was about five at the time, and, despite the fact that he had become a very good swimmer because of those daily outings, Mother still made him wear a life jacket. Back then it was one of those big, bulky orange jackets that we called "water wings."

There was a large concrete platform out in the middle of the pool with a diving board, and it was fun to see who could hold his breath and swim under the platform from one side to the other. However, on one of our daily swims my brother decided to swim underwater the full length of the platform.

Family fun often involved swimming at a pool or lake.

He intended to start from the deep end of the diving board, swim underwater to the steps on the other end, go under the bottom rung, and come up on the other side. That meant when he got to the steps he had to pull himself down to that last rung—life jacket and all—by holding onto the underwater ladder and forcing himself down by sheer strength. Without a life jacket that little adventure would probably have been OK, but when he tried to force himself under that last step, the life jacket caught and trapped him three feet under the water.

Our little sister, who was two years younger than our brother, kept saying, "Where is Bubba?" When someone finally got around to paying attention to what she was saying, the panic was on. We began looking everywhere for him in that giant pool. Now this was not a pool like one you would see today—you couldn't see the bottom because of the greenish, strong-smelling water. But it was my father who finally caught a faint glimpse of the orange life jacket through that murky sulfur water and dove down, working frantically until he was able to get the jacket dislodged. He had to literally push him farther down in the water to free the jacket from the steps before he could bring him up.

No one knew for sure how long he had been under the water, but it had to have been several minutes. He had already held his breath for the time it took to swim lengthwise under the platform, the time it took to force himself under the steps, the time it took for him to be missed, and then the time it took for my father to get him out of the trap. When my brother was asked if he was scared, he answered, "No, I knew my daddy would come and get me out of the trap, but I didn't like it when he pushed me farther under the water—I wanted up."

The reason I am sharing this story is because it is a perfect example of how we should look to our heavenly Father every time we feel trapped. If we pray and put our trust in God, He will rescue us from the traps that Satan has laid for us. And we also have to trust God and not get into fear when there are things we don't understand. Remember, it was hard for a five-year-old to understand why his dad was pushing him farther down in the water, but that was the only way to get him out of the trap.

Our heavenly Father will never do anything except what is best for us. God not only delivers us from the snare laid by the trapper (Satan), but according to the last part of verse 3, He also delivers us from the deadly *pestilence*. I always thought a pestilence was something that attacked crops—bugs, locusts, grasshoppers, spider mites, mildew, or root rot. After doing a word study on the word *pestilence*, however, I found, to my surprise that pestilence attacks people—not crops!

Pestilence is "any virulent or fatal disease; an epidemic that hits the masses of people." These deadly diseases attach themselves to a person's body with the intent to destroy it. But God tells us in verse 3 that He will deliver us from these deadly diseases.

God put this preventive promise in verse 3 for you to stand on for protection from both ways in which harm can destroy a life. Train yourself to stop during the split second when temptation rears its ugly head. Say aloud: "God delivers me from the snare of the trapper—that thing that makes me lose my temper, that lust that tries to rise up in my heart, that person who constantly offends me, that critical word that comes flying out of my mouth in a heated moment, and that situation that always causes me to get frustrated."

I don't know too many people who have thought of Psalm 91 as a good scriptural promise to keep someone from getting caught in the trap of repetitive sin or who realize how to push back and proclaim that God has delivered them from harm. This verse tells about the double deliverance from these traps.

What good would it do to be delivered from harm—only to be caught in a sin that destroys us? And, on the other hand, what good would it do to be delivered from a sin—only to be destroyed by a deadly pestilence? Thank God this verse covers both. A parent's daily prayer should be thanksgiving to God that our children are delivered from sin and they are delivered from deadly diseases. What a gift—but an unused gift can be deadly.

Chapter

UNDER HIS WINGS

> He will cover you with His pinions,
> and under His wings you may seek
> refuge.
>
> —PSALM 91:4

WHEN YOU PICTURE A magnificent flying bird, it is usually not a chicken that comes to mind. I've never seen a chicken portrayed in flight—many eagles, but no chickens. We quote Isaiah 40:31, which talks about being borne up on the wings of eagles or with wings like eagles. There is a difference, however, between being *on* His wings and being *under* His wings. This promise in Psalm 91 is not elaborating on the *flying* wing—but on the *sheltering* wing. One indicates *strength* and *accomplishment*, while the other denotes *protection* and *familiarity*. When you imagine the warmth of a nest and the security of being under the wings of the nurturing love of a mother hen with chicks, it paints a vivid picture of the sheltering wing of God's protection that the psalmist refers to in this passage.

Is everyone protected under the wings? Did you notice that it says, "He will cover you with His pinions [feathers], and under His wings you *may* seek refuge"? Again, it's up to us to make that decision! We can seek refuge under His wings if we *choose* to.

Children at a very early age should be taught to seek protection under the wings of the Almighty. We, as parents, have authority for the well-being of our children when they are in the home and under our covering. And we still have a certain amount of authority over our children all of their lives, but once they become of age, they need to be taught to make this covenant personal and remain under the wings of the Almighty by their own volition.

The Lord gave me a vivid picture of what it means to seek refuge under His wings, and I have found that this illustration brings particular understanding and insight in the hearts of our children. My husband, Jack, and I live out in the country, and one spring our old mother hen hatched a brood of baby chickens. One afternoon when they were scattered all over the yard, I suddenly saw the shadow of a hawk overhead. Then I noticed something that taught me a lesson I will never forget. That mother hen did not run to those little chicks and jump on top of them to try to cover them with her wings. No!

Instead she squatted down, spread out her wings, and began to cluck. And those little chickens, from every direction, came running *to her* to get under those outstretched wings. Then the hen pulled her wings down tight, tucking every little chick safely under her. To get to those babies, the hawk would have to go through the mother.

When I think of those baby chicks running to their mother, I realize it is under His wings that we *may* seek refuge—but we have to run to Him. "He will cover you with His pinions, and under His wings you may seek refuge." That one little word *may* is a strong word! Our children need to be taught that it is up to us! All that mother hen did was cluck and expand her wings to tell her chicks where to come. This verse shows the maternal hovering side to His protection:

> Like flying birds so the Lord of hosts
> will protect Jerusalem.
> He will protect and deliver it;
> He will pass over and rescue it.

> Return to Him from whom you have
> deeply defected, O sons of Israel.
>
> —ISAIAH 31:5–6

> Jerusalem, Jerusalem...How often I wanted to gather your children together, the way a hen gathers her chicks under her wings, and you were unwilling.
>
> —MATTHEW 23:37

It is interesting that Jesus uses the correlation of *maternal* love to demonstrate His attachment to us. There is a certain fierceness to motherly love we cannot overlook. God is deeply committed to us—yet at the same time *we can reject* His outstretched arms if we so choose. It is available but not automatic.

God does not run here and there, trying to cover us. He said, "I have made protection possible. You run to Me!" And when we do run to Him in faith, *the enemy*, then, has *to go through God to get to us!* Jesus often used illustrations to put across a point, and what a vivid picture this gives us of our Father's protection.

Chapter

A MIGHTY FORTRESS IS MY GOD

> His faithfulness is a shield and bulwark.
>
> —Psalm 91:4

I WANT YOU TO PICTURE a big shield out in front of you—one so big that you can hide behind it and no one can even see you. That shield is God Himself. *Your faith in those promises and in God's faithfulness to do what He says becomes a shield* in front of you to protect you from dangerous things with which the enemy tries to hurt you.

When you are not behind the shield, the enemy can see you and hurt you. You will also find yourself out from behind the shield when you *forget* about God's promises or get into a lot of fear. One of the enemy's biggest tricks is to whisper fearful thoughts not only in our minds as parents but also in the minds of our children. We need to teach our children that when those thoughts come, they can ward off his attack by saying, "My faith is strong because I know my God is faithful, and His faithfulness is my shield!"

How often I've heard people say, "I can't dwell in the shelter of God. I mess up and fall short too many times. I feel guilty and unworthy." God knows all about our weaknesses. Our children need to be taught that they can no more earn or deserve this protection than they can earn or deserve their salvation. The main thing is that if we slip and fall, we must not stay lying down. Get up, repent, and get back under that shield of protection. Thankfully this verse says it is His faithfulness, not ours, that is our shield.

> If we are faithless, He remains faithful, for
> He cannot deny Himself.
>
> —2 Timothy 2:13

This was the case with my husband. God certainly showed His faithfulness over Jack when he was seven years old. All of the people who worked for his father had taken their boats to Lake Brownwood to do some night fishing. Jack was placed in a boat with five adults so he would be well supervised. Since one of the men in the boat was an expert swimmer, his mother and dad thought he would be in especially good hands.

Jack at age seven on the fishing trip

Later that night, during one of the times when the boats were going back and forth to shore for bait, Jack had gotten out of his boat and into another one without anyone noticing. Then off they went—without Jack—back onto the lake in the dark. This was back before there were rules about life jackets and lights on your fishing boats, so no one could see in the dark what actually happened. Perhaps they hit a stump. But for some reason the boat Jack had been in sank. All five of the people in it drowned, even the expert swimmer. I believe it was the plan of the enemy to kill Jack at a young age, but God had other plans.

Michele Hargrove, mother of three from Houston, Texas, tells of her family's experience of God's shield of protection over her twelve-year-old son, Ross, during a winter skiing vacation. She tells the story here.

> Our kids are a little older (nineteen, fifteen, and twelve), so they enjoyed skiing at times on this trip without us. It was on the sixth day that I just happened to look up on a slope and saw the three of them going up a lift. We got their attention and then all met at the top. After visiting for a while, we made plans to meet up later for lunch, and all took off down the mountain (my husband and I together and the kids all together). About halfway down the mountain I came upon my husband in the middle of the slope, hollering, and there was all kinds of commotion going on. My son lay crumpled at the base of a tree.
>
> 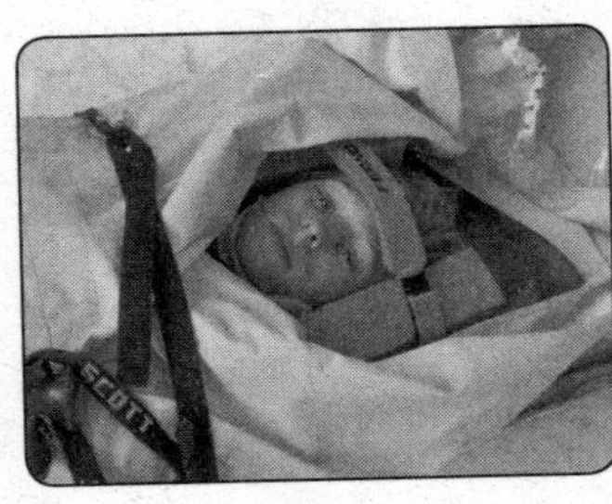
>
> Ross Hargrove
>
> He was hit by a huge man (at least 200 pounds) who was going full blast down the mountain and ran into my son. Ross is a small kid for his age. He weighs around 75 pounds soaking wet! My husband saw the impact and saw the man hit him, then he saw Ross *helicopter* through the air and hit a

tree! The man was standing when I came up, but only seconds later he went unconscious. If you have never skied, the speed that you can get up to heading down a mountain at full blast can do a great deal of damage. As my husband and I came upon our son, he tried to sit up, and his arm was dangling in a very sickening and unnatural position. When paramedics arrived, I backed away and took my two daughters by the hand, and we prayed Psalm 91 out loud over Ross. After they loaded him behind a sled, I was able to ride the snowmobile that dragged him down the hill.

I prayed this psalm continuously, over and over, as we headed for the ambulance. Not only was I worried about the arm, but also there was concern for neck and head injuries as well. We were rushed to the hospital, and after X-rays and CAT scans were done on him, we were given his condition—not a bone broken, not a thing wrong with him! He was released, and although he was sore and a little bruised, he was fine. My husband and I both insisted on further tests for his arm because we had both seen it dangling and just knew it had to be broken. But God answered our prayer and healed him completely! I

> feel it was a miracle that we just happened to see them on that huge mountain with tons of lifts. It was a blessing that we were there with them and could help them all cope through such a horrific ordeal. It was a miracle that my tiny son came out fine while this huge man ended up with many problems and a long stay in the hospital.
>
> ...My son is only twelve, but he has a powerful testimony that he can now use to help people understand the love of God and the power of prayer and God's covenant promise. God is so good![1]

Note that this verse in Psalm 91:4 declares God's faithfulness to us as both a shield and a bulwark in a double-layered analogy. The passage uses two military symbols of fortification and protection. God is our bulwark, our tower—our wall of protection in a collective sense, and He is also our shield—a very individualized defense. This verse indicates *double* protection.

Chapter

I WILL NOT FEAR the TERROR

You will not be afraid of the terror by night.

—Psalm 91:5

It is interesting to note that verses 5 and 6 of Psalm 91 cover an entire twenty-four-hour period, emphasizing *day-and-night* protection. But what is more important is that these two verses encompass *every evil known to man*.

The psalmist divides the list into four categories. We will look at those categories one at a time. The first, *terror by night*, includes all the evils that come through man: kidnapping, robbery, rape, murder, terrorism, and wars. Few parents have escaped the fear—or horror—or alarm of something happening to one of their children. What parent has ever read a newspaper article of some child being kidnapped without having a chill of fear run up his spine at the thought of his child being abducted? God knows the fears that face parents; that is why He says, "You will not be afraid of any of those things, because they will not approach you." The first thing verse 5 deals with is fear.

Over and over Jesus told us, "Do not fear!" Why do you think He continually reminds us not to be afraid? Because it is through faith in His Word we are protected—and since fear is the opposite of faith, the Lord knows fear will keep us from operating in the faith that is necessary to receive. It is no wonder God addresses *the fear of terror* first.

Fear comes when we think we are responsible for bringing about this protection ourselves. Too often we think, "Oh, if I can just believe hard enough, maybe I'll be protected!" Practically every parent I have ever known has tried to reason out some protection plan for every possible vulnerable position in which his child might find himself. I hate to burst anyone's bubble, but one can never think of ways to cover every base in the natural. That's wrong thinking! God wants us to realize that the protection is already there.

Protection has already been provided, whether we receive it or not. Faith is simply the *choice to receive* what Jesus has *already* done. The Bible gives classic examples of how to deal with terror.

The answer is in the blood of Jesus. Exodus 12:23 tells us that when Israel put blood on the door facings, the destroyer could not come in. The animal blood they used serves as a *type* and *shadow*, or a picture of the blood of Jesus that ratifies our *better* protection—under our *better* covenant (Heb. 8:6).

When I confess aloud, "My child is covered and protected by the blood of Jesus"—and believe it, the devil literally cannot come in. Remember Psalm 91:2 tells us, "I will say to the Lord, 'My refuge and my fortress.'" I have said this before, but it bears repeating: it is *heart and mouth*—believing with our heart and confessing with our mouth.

If we find ourselves afraid of the *terror by night*, that is our barometer letting us know we are not dwelling and abiding close to the Lord in the shelter of the Most High and believing His promises for us and our children. Fear comes in when we are confessing things other than what God has said. When our eyes are not on God, fear will come. But let that fear be a reminder to repent.

> We walk by faith, not by sight.
>
> —2 Corinthians 5:7

We have to choose to believe His Word more than we believe what we see—more than we believe the terror attack. It's not that we deny the existence of the attack, for the attack may be very real. But God wants our faith in His Word to become more of a reality to us than what we see in the natural.

For example, the law of gravity is a fact! No one denies the existence of gravity, but just as the laws of aerodynamics can temporarily supersede the law of gravity, Satan's attacks can also be superseded by a higher law—the law of faith and obedience to God's Word. Faith does not deny the existence of *terror.* There are simply higher laws in the Bible for overcoming it.

David did not deny the existence of the giant. Fear has us compare the size of the giant to ourselves. Faith, on the other hand, had David compare the size of the giant to the size of his God. David's eyes saw *the giant,* but his faith saw *the promises* (1 Sam. 17).

Over the years as a pastor's wife I can recall countless people who called my husband and me in an emergency situation for help. Also I remember the times when God miraculously healed the broken neck of Audra's son, Skylar, after he fell from his bike...when Jennifer McCullough's missionary village was overtaken by murderers...when Mary Johnson was kidnapped and trapped in an abandoned cabin. God's promise in Psalm 91 turned every one of those potential disasters into victory. They were all close friends, and we were thrilled to have been personally involved, even though we were praying for those miracles from a distance.

But none compare to those times when the terror is brought right in your front door. Julee Sherrick experienced such a time and tells of God's miraculous intervention. Her parents are God-fearing pastors who stand daily on the Psalm 91 promises for the protection of their children. One particular Sunday morning Julee was getting ready for church when she heard a knock. Startled to have a large man shove his way into the apartment, Julee started using the Word of God as her defense. In the natural there was no way for a young girl to escape from a strong man, but her parents had trained her to be so confident in her covenant promise that she stood firm and never gave up.

Julee told me her story in her own words:

> It did not take long for me to realize that the man's intention was rape. I remember thinking, "Things like this don't happen to me. I must be dreaming." He pushed me into my bedroom and onto the bed. We wrestled on the bed for what seemed to be about ten minutes. My emotions were

hysterical, but my spirit was strong and I kept saying, "Jesus, help me; Jesus, help me." The man kept telling me to shut up, but I said, "I don't know who you are or what you have done, or even if the police are after you, but you need Jesus. I am going to church today, and you can come." When I would say things like that to him, he would momentarily snap out of his stupor. Then a demonic look would come over his face and he would start after me again. And I would begin calling out to Jesus and confessing His promises.

Julee Sherrick

It took forty-five minutes of spiritual battle as he came at me time after time, but I never quit calling out to Jesus and quoting His promises. And each time it would bring confusion and immobility on him—thwarting every attempted attack. Then, during one of those times when he was at a standstill, I was able to get out the door and escape unharmed. Later, after he was apprehended and held in custody, I found out that he had sexually

> assaulted numerous young women, and I was the only one who had been able to escape without harm. I thank God for His covenant of protection, but we have to believe it and put it to work. It certainly saved my life that day.[1]

As parents we have no way of knowing the extent of protection we extend to our children when we use our authority and fill them with the knowledge of the promises God has made in Psalm 91. We do not have to be afraid of the terror *of what man can do to harm us*. One of the biggest areas we fear as parents is having someone harm our child. God knew that and provided us with the strongest protection promise imaginable—that the terror won't come near us. What a powerful assurance!

Chapter

I WILL NOT FEAR the ARROW

You will not be afraid... of the arrow that flies by day.

—Psalm 91:5

The second category of evil is the *arrow that flies by day*. Practically every child knows about arrows; therefore it is easy to teach them that there are arrows in the spiritual realm that do more than hurt us physically.

Arrows can be sent to hurt your body *physically*, but they can also be sent to hurt your feelings *emotionally* or to pull you away from God *spiritually*.

The enemy sends these arrows on purpose and tries to aim them at the spot that will hurt the most. Some arrows are like a temptation to get you to sin—perhaps in an area where you're still losing your temper, where maybe you're selfish, where you get your feelings hurt too easily, or where you are still into fear. Think about some areas where you are not very strong in God's Word. Those will often be the main target.

This category indicates we are in a *spiritual* battle zone; arrows are deliberately sent by the enemy and meticulously *aimed at the spot that will cause the most damage*. The enemy seldom attacks us in an area where we are built up and strong. He attacks us where we're still struggling. That's why we have to run to God! And when we do battle using our spiritual weapons, the enemy's arrows will not approach us.

In Ephesians 6:16 God tells us that we have a "shield of faith with which [we] will be able to extinguish all the flaming arrows of the evil one." This covers the area of intentional danger. The arrows are aimed on purpose and released. These are not regular, everyday arrows; they are *on fire*. Yet God doesn't say we can miss most of them. He says we can extinguish *all* of them. When arrows are sent to wound us spiritually, physically, mentally, emotionally, or financially, God wants us to ask and believe by faith that He will *pick us up* and deliver us from calamity. Few children know that they can be picked up out of the pathway of harm. That is why it is so important for them to be taught.

But there are also demonic arrows that come our way in the form of accidental occurrences that can inflict great harm upon us—such as the electrical fire that starts in the wall of a home, the blown tire on the freeway, or the fall down a flight of stairs. Our granddaughter Jolena and her daughter, Peyton, experienced that miraculous protection on a day at home that started out like any other, before they felt the arrow of an unexpected accident. Jolena tells the story:

> I am a busy mom of three, so I am often in a hurry to get somewhere. On this particular day I was rushing out the door to take photos for a friend. My husband was in the garage with the garage door open. I had told our three children—ages seven, five, and three—to stay inside the house and play and that I would be right back; if they needed something, their daddy was in the garage. So I jumped in

Peyton and Jolena

the car, put it in reverse, and tuned out the rest of the world.

This is the exact moment that the miracle happened: my minivan window was up, my mind was focused on what I had to do, and any anxiety inside of me was being quieted because I had left my children safely upstairs. As I hurriedly pulled out of the driveway, suddenly I heard my husband's friend, Matt, yelling at me to stop! He and my husband were running toward the van, hollering Peyton's name! To my absolute horror I realized that my daughter had run outside, climbed on her bike, and driven it behind my van. As I had backed out, she was knocked over and had grabbed hold of the bumper.

You can imagine the agony of our five-year-old child as she clung for her very life to the bumper that was backing over her. Even though I was looking back over my shoulder rather than trusting my rearview mirror, she was too far below the back window to be noticed. It is pointless to say that there is a major blind spot in a minivan. She had ridden behind my van without my seeing her. By the time I stopped, it was too late—she had been thrown down under the back of the minivan.

> In what was measured by seconds, but is a parent's eternity and anguish beyond words, neither I nor Heath nor Matt knew what to expect. She was lying on the ground under the back of our van, with her head in the direct line of the rear tire. The bike was under the car tire, totally demolished, and Peyton was under her fallen bike. One second more and life as we knew it would have ended forever.
>
> Her bicycle was crunched beyond repair. As I picked her up off of the ground, I was praying and checking her out all in one movement to see if she had been harmed in any way! She calmly looked at me and said, "It's OK, Mom, I'm not hurt, but I think I'm going to need a new bike." And truly, there was not a scratch on her! I held her and gave thanks and praise to God. I couldn't see my daughter, but God sees everything, and He put someone there to see her and yell at me just in time! I thank God for our Psalm 91 covenant of protection.[1]

We have a *covenant* with God telling us *not to be afraid of the arrow that flies by day.* Assignments will rise up, but we are told not to be afraid of the arrows. He has promised they will not hit their target.

Chapter

I WILL NOT BE AFRAID of the PESTILENCE

You will not be afraid...of the pestilence that stalks in darkness.

—Psalm 91:5–6

SINCE THERE ARE so many horrible diseases in the world, it is easy to think that it's normal to be sick. Sometimes it is hard, though, to believe these promises in Psalm 91, because we see so many sick people in the world.

It is so important to renew our thinking until

our thoughts line up with the Bible. Matthew 8:16 says that many people were brought to Jesus, and He healed all who were sick. Then verse 17 says that He did these things to make come true what Isaiah the prophet said: "He Himself took our infirmities and carried away our diseases." If He bore it for us, we don't have to bear it again.

Even if the world doesn't believe in the healing power of Jesus, that does not keep it from being true. Some people think that faith is hard, but that is because they think faith is a "feeling." *Faith is not a feeling. Faith is simply choosing to believe what God says in His Word and refusing to doubt.*

Pestilence is the only evil God names twice in Psalm 91. Since God doesn't waste words, He must have a specific reason for repeating this promise. When we tell our children something more than once, it is usually because we really want them to hear us. God knew the pestilence and the fear that would be running rampant in these last days. The world is teeming with fatal epidemics hitting people by the thousands, so God catches our attention by repeating this promise.

It's as though God is saying, "I said in verse 3, 'You are delivered from the deadly pestilence, but did you really hear Me? Just to be sure, I am saying it again in verse 6: '*You do not have to be afraid of the deadly pestilence*'!"

Our son, Bill, was born with a serious membrane

disease in his lungs. We were alarmed because it was the same disease that had, just a short time before Bill was born, killed President Kennedy's baby, who was surrounded with some of the best doctors in America.

None of the hospital staff expected Bill to live, and he was placed in an incubator for over a month. Every day we would go to the hospital just to watch him through a huge glass window. It was a hard time, but somehow, God gave my husband and me a gift of faith to believe Psalm 91 that he would live and not die.

It is so amazing to see all the different ways in which God works mysteriously when you are trusting in His Word. Our little hometown doctor was definitely sent by God. Two of his nephews had died from that same disease, and he had quit practicing medicine for a while to study and try to find a cure for it. In fact, the doctor had only recently returned to practicing medicine when Bill was born. So when he discovered that Bill had the exact same disease his nephews had, he started trying everything on Bill he had read about during his studies. And miraculously Bill started responding to one of the treatments.

Thanks be to God for this promise—for it is He who delivers us from the deadly pestilence. Instead of losing our baby, we were able to bring home a perfectly healed, healthy baby boy from the hospital.

Whatever you are believing for...whatever you are going though...Psalm 91 speaks of the protection available to us from all the fatal diseases (pestilence) that are in the world around us. We thank Jesus for what He did on the cross for each one of us and for His wonderful promises in Psalm 91.

Bill, home at last

The pestilence mentioned in Psalm 91:6 is spelled out in detail in the curses listed in Deuteronomy 28, where more forms of pestilence are named than one can imagine. Thank God for His promise in Galatians 3:13 that tells us we are *redeemed* from the curse.

Luke 21:11 states that one of the signs of the end times is an outbreak of pestilence. And today we have many widespread diseases such as AIDS, cancer, malaria, heart disease, tuberculosis, and on and on; then you can add to that list the horrible disasters that hit all over the world. But no matter what pestilence we or our children might be facing, God has declared: "You will not be afraid...of the pestilence that stalks in darkness...*it shall not approach you*" (Ps. 91:5–7, emphasis added).

Chapter

I WILL NOT FEAR the DESTRUCTION

You will not be afraid...of the destruction that lays waste at noon.

—Psalm 91:5–6

This fourth category of evil is *destruction*. Destruction encompasses the *evils over which mankind has no control*—those things the world ignorantly calls *acts of God*—tornadoes, floods, hail, hurricanes, or fire! God very plainly tells us we are not to fear destruction. These natural disasters are not from God.

In Mark 4:39 Jesus rebuked the storm, and it

became perfectly calm. This demonstrates that God is not the author of such things; otherwise, Jesus would never have contradicted His Father by rebuking something sent by Him.

There is no place in the natural you can go and be safe from every *destruction*—every natural disaster. We can never anticipate what might come when we least expect it. But no matter where you are in the world, God says to run to His shelter, and you can be protected.

Our granddaughter Jolena and her husband, Heath Adams, were stationed in Turkey just before the war was declared in Iraq. Soon after her arrival in Turkey, Jolena started working as a lifeguard at a pool. One day at the end of June she began to hear a loud noise that sounded much like a plane breaking the sound barrier; then everything started to shake. Everyone around her began to panic when the water splashed in the pool from an earthquake, which was later found to be a 6.3 on the Richter scale. Swimmers tried desperately to get out of the water to find some place of safety, while children clung to Jolena and screamed in fear. Everywhere people were hollering, but Jolena said she felt a peace and a calm come over her. She started praying Psalm 91 in a loud voice, pleading the blood of Jesus over the children at the pool, over

Jolena Adams

her home, and over the air force base. Suddenly everyone around her became perfectly quiet and listened to her pray. No one at the pool or on the base was seriously hurt, but just five minutes away more than a thousand people were killed in the quake.

Did you know that every evil known to man will fall into one of these four categories we have named in chapters 6 through 9 (verses 5 and 6 of Psalm 91)—terror, arrows, pestilence, or destruction? And the amazing thing is that God has offered us deliverance from them all.

This psalm is not filled with exceptions or vague conditions as if trying to give God an out or an excuse to fail to fulfill the promises. Rather, it is a bold statement of what He *wants* to do for us.

We can receive anything God has already provided. The secret is in knowing that everything for which God has made provision is clearly spelled out and defined in the Word of God. *If you can find where God has offered it, you can have it!* Our children need to be taught that it is never God holding it back. His provision is already there—waiting to be received.

God is faithful to all the promises He has made. He didn't create man and then leave man to himself. When He created us, He automatically made Himself responsible to care for us and meet our every need. And when He makes a promise, He is faithful to what He has promised.

Faith is not a tool to manipulate God into giving you something *you* want. Faith is simply the means by which we accept what God has already made available. Our goal needs to be the *renewal* of our minds to such an extent that we have more faith in God's Word than in what we perceive with our physical senses. God does not make promises that are out of our reach.

When the Lord first began showing me these promises, and my mind was still struggling with, "How can this be?"—*doubts*—He took me to a portion of His Word that helped to set me free:

> What then? If some did not believe, their unbelief will not nullify the faithfulness of God, will it? May it never be! Rather, let God be found true, though every man be found a liar, as it is written, "That you may . . . prevail when you are judged."
>
> —ROMANS 3:3–4

God is telling us that even though there may be some who *don't believe*, their unbelief will never nullify His promises to the ones who *do believe*. Paul in Romans, quoting from the Old Testament, gives us an important reminder that what we as individuals choose to believe and confess will cause us to prevail during a time of judgment.

Sometimes we find out about these things just

in the nick of time. Tanya Cliff wrote to say that she wished we could have seen the eyes of her children light up when boxes of my books were delivered to them! And the exciting thing is that the very next week several church families who had been standing on Psalm 91 had amazing testimonies after a terrible tornado. One of the families was right in the path of the tornado and no alarms had gone off in the area to give them warning. A neighbor testified to seeing the tornado approach their house, lift up and twirl around the roof, then pass them by. Most of the homes on the block were severely damaged or destroyed, but theirs was completely unharmed. Even the ladder leaning against the van in the driveway was intact! Destruction was headed straight for them, but they found out about God's promises just at the right time so they could stand.

Without the promises of protection throughout the Word of God, and especially without our Psalm 91 covenant—*listing all forms of protection made available in one psalm*—we might feel rather presumptuous if, on our own, we asked God to protect us from all the things listed in these last four verses. In fact, we probably would not have the nerve to ask for all of this coverage. But, praise God, He offered this protection to us before we even had a chance to ask!

Chapter

THOUGH a THOUSAND FALL

> A thousand may fall at your side and ten thousand at your right hand, but it shall not approach you.... For you have made the LORD, my refuge, even the Most High, your dwelling place.
>
> —PSALM 91:7, 9

THERE ARE SOME PEOPLE who don't know how to claim these promises. And sometimes it's hard to believe God's Word when you see people sick and dying all around you, but God tells you that not everyone is going to believe.

Do we even stop to consider what God is saying to us in verse 7? Do we have the courage to trust God's Word enough to believe *He means this literally*? Is it possible for this to be true and for us to miss out on these promises?

What an awesome statement God is making here in verse 7! God wants us to know that even though there will be a thousand falling by our side and ten thousand at our right hand, it does not negate the promise that destruction will not approach the one who chooses to believe and trust His Word. God means exactly what He says.

Disaster can strike suddenly when everything is going well, and it can really break your heart to see times when thousands fall. This is why the promises in Psalm 91 are so important to you.

It is no accident that the little statement "it shall not approach you" is tucked right here in the middle of the psalm. Have you noticed how easy it is to become fearful when disaster strikes all around you? We begin to feel as Peter must have felt when he walked on the water to Jesus. It is easy to see how he started sinking into the waves when he saw all the turbulence of the storm going on around him.

God knew there would be times when we would hear so many negative reports, see so many needs, and encounter so much danger around us that we would feel overwhelmed. That is why He warned us ahead of time that thousands would be falling all around us. He did not want us to be caught off guard. But at that point we have a choice to make. The ball is then in our court! We can either choose to run to His shelter in faith, and the storm will not approach us, or we can passively live our lives the way the world does, not realizing there is something we can do about it.

Psalm 91 is the *preventive* measure that God has given to His children against every evil known to mankind. No place else in the Word are all of the protection promises (including help from angels, as well as promises insuring our authority) accumulated in one covenant to offer such a total package for living in this world. It is both an *offensive* and *defensive measure* for warding off every evil before it has had time to strike. This is not only a *cure* but also a plan for *complete prevention*!

What tremendous insight after our minds have been renewed by the Word of God to realize, contrary to the world's thinking, we do not have to be among the ten thousand who fall at our right hand.

> You will only look on with your eyes
> And see the recompense of the wicked.
>
> —Psalm 91:8

Let's look for just a moment at this scripture with our faith in mind; do we sometimes fall short into unbelief? Faith in God, in His Son Jesus Christ, and in His Word is *counted* in God's eyes as righteousness. But when we are in unbelief, to a degree we are placing ourselves in the category of the *wicked*. Sometimes, even as a Christian, I have been an *unbelieving* believer when it comes to receiving *all* of God's Word.

Jesus says in Matthew 5:18, "Not the smallest letter or stroke shall pass from the Law until all is accomplished." Even if believers have never utilized this psalm in its full potential, the truth has never passed away or lost one ounce of its power.

Many people think of the gospel as an insurance policy, securing only their eternity and their comfort after disaster strikes. They are depriving themselves of so much. Perhaps we all need to ask ourselves the question "What kind of coverage do I have—fire or life?" God's Word is more than merely an escape from hell; it is a handbook for living a victorious life *in this world*.

Have you ever been really frightened when you heard the weather report that a tornado was over your town? Late one night we turned on our radio just as they reported that a tornado was on the ground right behind the country club. That's where we live.

We could see several of the React Club vehicles parked on the road below our hill as the members watched the funnel cloud that seemed to be headed straight for our house. Some of our son's friends were visiting, and to their surprise, Jack quickly ordered our family to get outside with our Bibles (even though we were in our pajamas) and start circling the house—quoting Psalm 91 and taking authority over the storm. Jack had the children speaking directly to the storm, just as Jesus did. The sky was a strange color; everything was still, and not a night creature was making a sound. There was so much electricity in the air that our hair felt like it was standing on end.

The eerie silence suddenly turned into a roar, with torrents of rain coming down in what seemed like bucketsful. Finally Jack had a peace the danger had passed, even though, by sight, nothing had changed.

We walked back into the house just in time to hear the on-location reporter call the radio announcer and exclaim over the air, with so much excitement he was almost shouting, "This is nothing short of a miracle—the funnel cloud south of the Brownwood Country Club has suddenly lifted up and vanished into the clouds."

You should have seen those kids jumping and hollering. It was the first time my son's friends had observed the supernatural at work. However, their surprise was no greater than that of my daughter's college professor the next day. He asked the students in his class what they were doing during the storm. Several said they were in the bathtub under a mattress. Some were in closets, and one was in a storm cellar!

You can imagine the astonishment when he got around to our daughter, Angelia, who said, "With the tornado headed our direction, my family was circling the house, quoting from Psalm 91: We will not be afraid...of the destruction that lays waste...a thousand will fall at your side, ten thousand at your right hand, but it will *not approach us...No evil will befall you, nor will any plague or calamity come near your dwelling*."

People in the world call what we experienced a lucky break, but that is not luck. God honors His Word when we believe it and act on it. Some people just do not know about the protection of the Lord.

It is important to realize that there is a difference between the destruction of the enemy and persecution for the gospel's sake. Paul writes in 2 Timothy 3:12, "All who desire to live godly in Christ Jesus will be persecuted." Our children need to be taught that there are times when we will be mistreated because of our stand for the cause of Christ. Psalm 91 is a very distinct concept dealing with natural disasters, accidents, sickness, and destruction. Jesus suffered persecution, but He did not face calamity, disaster, and mishap. Accidents never even *approached* Him. This distinction is easy to understand if you separate persecution from freak accidents and mishaps.

There is a place where calamity literally does not even approach us.

Too many people see Psalm 91 as a beautiful promise that they file right alongside all of their other quality reading material. It makes them feel comforted every time they read it. But I do not want anyone to read this book and fail to see the *superior significance* to these promises in this psalm. These are not written for our inspiration but for our protection. These are not words of comfort *in* affliction but words of deliverance *from* affliction.

Chapter

NO PLAGUE COMES NEAR MY FAMILY

> There shall no evil befall you, nor any plague or calamity come near your tent.
>
> —Psalm 91:10, AMP

Sometimes it is hard not to worry about your family. Have you ever been tormented with the thought that your spouse might die? Or, perhaps, a child! That is a horrible feeling, and God does not want you to be in that kind of fear. That is why in verse 10 He tells you that *no disaster will come to your family.* It is at this point in the psalm that the Bible makes this covenant more than merely being about ourselves!

God has just added a *new dimension* to the promise—the opportunity to exercise faith not only for ourselves but also for the protection of our entire household. If these promises were only available to us as individuals, they would not be completely comforting. Because God has created within us both an instinct to be protected and a need to protect those who belong to us, He has assured us here that these promises are for each of us and our *households.*

It appears that the Old Testament leaders had a better understanding of this concept than we who are under the new covenant. That is why Joshua chose for himself *and for his household.*

> If it is disagreeable in your sight to serve the LORD, choose for yourselves today whom you will serve...but as for me *and my house*, we will serve the LORD.
>
> —JOSHUA 24:15, EMPHASIS ADDED

As Joshua made the decision that his household would serve God with him, he was influencing their destiny and declaring their protection at the same time. In much the same way Rahab bargained with the Israeli spies for her whole family (Josh. 2:13).

When our hearts are truly steadfast and we are trusting in His faithfulness to fulfill His promises, we will not be constantly afraid something bad will happen to one of our family members.

> He will not fear evil tidings;
> His heart is steadfast, trusting in the
> Lord.
>
> —Psalm 112:7

Negative expectations will begin to pass away, and we will start expecting good reports. According to this verse we can grab our ears and proclaim, "These ears were made to hear good tidings!" The fear of bad tidings can plague our very existence, things like the fear of the phone ringing in the night, the fear of that knock on the door, of the siren of an ambulance, or of that letter of condolence. This verse promises that a steadfast heart will not live in constant fear of tragic news. Someone once said, "Fear knocked at the door and faith answered. No one was there."[1] When fear knocks, let your mouth say aloud, "I will not fear evil tidings; my heart is steady, trusting in You!"

Mama Ruth

God is faithful to watch over

us using every means possible. My mother-in-law, Ruth, became very good friends with Rocky, a three-year-old boxer dog who belonged to her next-door neighbors. She and Rocky would "chat" over the fence that separated their backyards, and whenever Grandmother Ruth was outside, Rocky seemed to know even if he was inside and would bark until someone let him out. One night, shortly after dark, Rocky began to whine and cry, scratching at the front door. When he refused to settle down, his owners finally decided to let him outside, but he kept coming back and whining louder than ever. He absolutely would not stop until he got one of them to go out, when they heard my eighty-seven-year-old mother-in-law crying for help. She had fallen in her back yard and couldn't get up.

It turned out to be a very cold night—one that Ruth might not have survived had she been left on the wet ground all night. When she heard the neighbors close their doors for the night, she said she thought about what a horrible way this was to end up, and she began crying out to the Lord to help her and reminding Him of her covenant. When the neighbors had put their boxer in for the night, he just would not settle down and continued to loudly bark until they unlocked their back door and

Rocky

he was able to get help for his friend. There is no end to God's ways and means of providing protection for those who trust His Word.

In Matthew 13:32 Jesus makes reference to the mustard seed starting as an herb but growing into a tree with the birds nesting in the branches. Others can find protection in our faith as well when we plant the seed of the Word. Not all His families are traditional families; sometimes the Lord puts a family back together by faith.

Foster Brother Family Miracle

A favorite story that warms my heart every time I think of it is the story of the Velez brothers who were all sent to different foster homes at a young age. The father had been sent to prison for molesting the boys, and the mother had died when the boys were little. No one wanted to take all the boys, so they were separated and sent in four different directions. Throughout his growing-up years Gilbert, next to the oldest, had fantasized of one day being reunited with his brothers. That, of course, was an impossibility; where were they? Surely by now even their names had changed. The Velez story intersected with ours during this time period.

Angie and David's college group was very evangelical. It was a common occurrence to find several of the group out in the streets every weekend leading people to Christ. On one of those occasions two of the guys ran into Gilbert Velez, who was now twenty and living alone. They led him in the prayer of salvation and invited him to come to one of their college Bible studies. The next meeting Gilbert was one of the first to arrive, blending into the group as though he had always been there. The group threw Gilbert in the van and took him on the spring break mission trip to Mexico. He told everyone about his separated brothers and how he believed he would one day have them all together again. Gilbert began devouring the Bible, and he found the story of Hannah in 1 Samuel, chapter 1. When he read that Hannah promised God that if He would give her a child, she would give him back to the Lord, Gilbert took that as a word from God. He told the Lord that if He would return his brothers to him, he would give them back to God.

A friend of his deceased mother wrote to a caseworker she knew in Dallas. Through a series of letters Gilbert found that one of his brothers, Jesse, had been in prison and after his release had been homeless on the streets of Dallas for three months. Even though Gilbert had been estranged from Jesse for six years, God supernaturally made a way for Jesse to move into the apartment with Gilbert, get involved in the college group, and give his life to Jesus.

Another series of difficult events opened the door for the next brother, Joseph, to be found in

Dallas and reunited with Gilbert and Jesse. God was on a roll. It was only a couple of months after that when they found their last brother, Samuel, in Fort Worth. When arrangements were made and it was time to pick Samuel up, Gilbert's car had broken down, but, as only God can do, a neighbor loaned the boys his Cadillac Escalade to make the trip in style.

Gilbert has played the role of mother and father, and true to the promise he made to God, he introduced each one of his brothers to the Lord. They all have jobs, some have taken college courses, they go on mission trips with the college group, and they pray their hearts out whenever someone has a need.

The night that I saw all four of the boys together for the first time, they were all dressed up in three-piece suits—looking like the King's kids that they are and out dressing every college kid around them.

On one of the college outings all four of the boys were in the same van headed to Miami to evangelize the Cubans in that area. It was on that trip that Jesse got separated from the group. Their phones were dead, and the boys were ready to panic—how could they find each other in those thousands of people? But they began to pray and claim God's promise

The Velez brothers

about lost sheep. God answered their prayers and reunited them in a tearful reunion again.

When it was his turn to preach at one of their college meetings, Jesse used the prodigal son story in Luke 15 as his text and told how God was faithful to find him, a prodigal son, in a lost and dying world and bring him home.

Gilbert has kept his promise. God gave him his brothers, and he has now given them back to God. How heartwarming it is to see them all together—loving and serving God.

The beauty of this psalm is that when someone prays for more than himself, he brings the entire family under the shield of God's Word. It introduces an added dimension to us as individuals to be able to apply the richness of this covenant to our entire household. We exercise a certain amount of authority for those *under our roof.*

A number of years ago Jack and I drove to the country with our son to feed sixty large, hungry Brahma cows. Bill took the sack of feed and started running in front of the cows as the feed poured out, but they didn't see the feed on the ground. They just saw Bill running with the feed sack on his shoulder, so they started chasing him. Jack and I were up on the top of the hill, and it looked like they all ran right over the top of him. The devil told me that he had been trampled to death like a cowboy in a stampede.

Fear came all over me, but then the Lord reminded me of this promise in Psalm 91:10. I started thanking God out loud that *I would not be afraid, because no tragedy would come near my family.* And God did a miracle. Even though those cows were running so fast that they couldn't stop, some way God parted the cows. They ran around Bill instead of over the top of him, and he was safe.

What a joy to know you have promises in Psalm 91 that will protect not only you but also those in your family and *near your dwelling*, as well.

Chapter

ANGELS ARE WATCHING OVER ME

> For He will give His angels charge concerning you, to guard you in all your ways. They will bear you up in their hands, that you do not strike your foot against a stone.
>
> —PSALM 91:11–12

IN VERSES 11 AND 12 God makes another unique promise concerning an additional dimension of our protection. This is one of the most precious promises of God, and He put it right here in Psalm 91. In fact, this is one of the promises Satan used to test Jesus.

Angels are spirits who serve God and are sent to help those who will receive salvation. Even though many Christians quote verses 11 and 12 as one of their favorite passages within Psalm 91, they give very little thought about the magnitude of what their families are escaping on a regular basis. Only after we get to heaven will we realize all the things from which we were spared because of the intervention of God's angels on our behalf.

Cullen at age five

When Cullen was five years old, he had quite an intervention while swimming with his cousins and a friend. One of the adults had said, "OK, everyone out of the pool."

Everyone else had headed inside the house when Cullen saw a plastic life raft come floating by. Wanting to impress the older friend, Cullen said, "Hey, watch this," as he stepped off the side of the pool onto the raft like it was a solid piece. It flipped out from under him, and he fell backward into the water, grazing his head on the side of the pool as he fell.

It was the deep end of the pool, and Cullen, with his arms and legs outstretched, just started sinking to the bottom. The boy dived in and grabbed him under the arms, but Cullen was unusually big for his age and weighed twice as much as the friend. Our son, Bill, had often said that Cullen felt like a chunk of lead when you tried to lift him, so the friend wondered if he would be able to get him to the top of the water—especially since he must have been dazed from scrapping his head on the concrete.

The friend knew they were in trouble, so he said that he called on God, and suddenly, he said, it felt like someone had grabbed him from behind under his armpits and began pushing both of them straight up from the bottom of the pool. (He thought one of the adults had seen them and dived in to help.) The boy said that suddenly he shot up out of the water with Cullen above him. Then he said it was like someone pulled Cullen from his arms and laid him on the side of the pool. (They were in water way over their heads, so he knew there was no way he could have lifted dead weight out of the pool.) Cullen started crying and coughing, and when the friend looked around, no one was there—absolutely, no one! It became obvious that *God had heard the call,* and He had sent help to *answer that call.*

A similar thing happened to Floyd, a close friend of ours who worked in the mines of Clovis, New Mexico. He had the responsibility of setting off the explosives. One particular day he was ready to push the switch when someone tapped him on the shoulder. To his surprise no one was anywhere around. Deciding it must have been his imagination, he prepared once again to detonate the dynamite, but he felt another tap on his shoulder. Again, no one was there. Floyd decided to move all the ignition equipment several hundred feet back up the tunnel. When he finally plunged the charger, the whole top of the tunnel caved in exactly where he had been standing. A coincidence? You could never make our friend believe that. He knew *someone* had tapped him on the shoulder.

We can all recall close calls where we escaped a tragedy and there was no explanation in the natural. It is possible to entertain angels without knowing it, as it says in Hebrews 13:2. Sadly, however, I believe most Christians have a tendency to disregard the ministry of angels altogether.

In 1968, while my brother-in-law was in the service, he and my sister and their new baby, Rhonda, were stationed in Fürth, Germany. For those of you who like to ride bicycles, you would have loved it there. Practically everyone rode bicycles everywhere they went, but the bikes in Germany—especially back in the 1960s—were not made for safety. Babies were carried in a

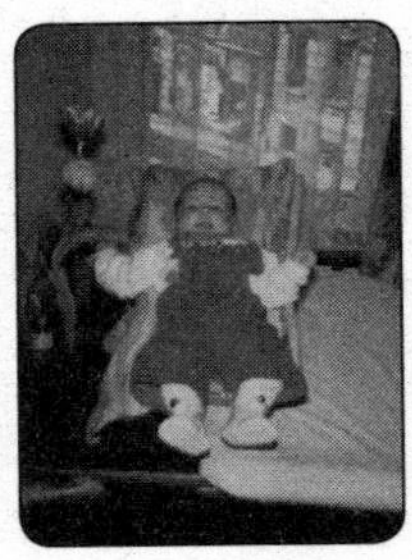

Rhonda in Germany

basket-type seat on the front of the bicycle with no cushions and no safety straps to hold them in. When Rhonda was nine months old, she was in the bike carrier as they crossed a very narrow railroad bridge with a pedestrian lane over the Regnitz River. It was pretty nerve-racking to drive a bike on that narrow walkway with the low side rails that gave very little protection from the fifty-foot drop to the water below, but no one would have dreamed of the real danger they were facing.

About halfway across, the front tire of the bike ran into the rail—throwing Rhonda head first out of the basket and over the railing. You can imagine the panic that would be surging through your body as you watched your baby flying through the air. But suddenly my sister's hand reached out over the rail—just in time to grab the little snowsuit that Rhonda was wearing. Another split second and she would have plunged to the water below, and there would have been no way to get off the bridge and down to the water in time to save her, even if she had survived the fall. God's angels were definitely on duty that day. No one has ever doubted those angels being right there—watching over that little one. Otherwise Rhonda would never have survived to be serving the Lord as she is today. How often she has been able to realize, "My life must count tremendously in God's eyes for Him to have saved me in such a miraculous way."

Are you in harm's way? Do you feel alone? You are not alone; God has given His angels—personal heavenly bodyguards—to protect you. More are fighting for you than against you.

Verse 11 of Psalm 91 says, "For He will give His angels *charge* concerning you." What does that mean? Think with me for a moment. Have you ever taken charge of a situation? When you take charge of something, you put yourself in a place of leadership. You begin telling everyone what to do and how to do it.

> Are they [angels] not all ministering spirits, sent out to render service for the sake of those who will inherit salvation?
>
> —Hebrews 1:14

When we look to God as the source of our protection and provision, the angels are constantly *rendering us aid* and *taking charge* of our affairs. Psalm 103:20 says, "...His angels, mighty in strength...obeying the voice of His Word!" As we proclaim God's Word, the angels hasten to carry it out.

> See that you do not despise one of these little ones, for I say to you that their angels in heaven continually see the face of My Father who is in heaven.
>
> —Matthew 18:10

Verse 11 of Psalm 91 continues, "...angels... *guard* you in all your ways." Have you ever seen a soldier standing guard, protecting someone? That soldier stands at attention—alert, watchful, and ready to protect at the first sign of attack. How much more will God's angels stand *guard* over God's children, alert and ready to protect them at all times? Do we believe that? Have we even thought about it? Faith is what releases this promise to work on our behalf. How comforting it is to know God has placed these heavenly guards to have charge over us.

Psalm 91 names so many different avenues through which God protects us. It is exciting to realize from this Old Testament psalm that protection is not just a random idea in God's mind—He is committed to it. Angelic protection is another one of the *unique* ways in which God has provided that protection. What an unusual idea to add actual beings designed to protect us. He has charged angels *to guard us in all our ways.*

Chapter

THE ENEMY IS UNDER MY FEET

> You will tread upon the lion and cobra, the young lion and the serpent ["dragon," KJV] you will trample down.
>
> —PSALM 91:13

DOES THIS VERSE MEAN that you really walk on top of a lion and over the head of a snake? Well, maybe on the mission field, but God is painting a picture so you can understand the *authority* you have.

My husband believes that too few Christians ever

use their authority. Too often they *pray* when they should be *taking authority*! If a gunman suddenly faced you, would you be confident enough in your authority that you could boldly declare, "I am in covenant with the living God, and I have a blood covering that protects me from anything you might attempt to do. So, in the name of Jesus, I command you to put down that gun"?

Let's look at what this verse is actually saying. What good does it do to have authority over lions and cobras unless we are in Africa or India or someplace like that? What *does* it mean when it says that we will tread on the lion, the young lion, the cobra, and the serpent (translated as "dragon" in the King James Version of the Bible)? These words are graphic representations of things that are potentially harmful in our daily lives. They amount to unforgettable ways of describing the different types of attacks that come against us. So, what do these terms mean to us today? Let's break them down.

1. Lion problems

First of all, we can encounter *lion problems*—these problems are bold, loud, forthright, and come out in the open to hit us head-on. At one time or another we have all had something blatant and overt come against us. It might have been a car wreck or a face-to-face encounter with the enemy during an outright attack on your health or life. It might have been an unexpected bill at the end of the month, causing a chain reaction of bounced checks. Those are *lion* problems—obvious difficulties that often seem insurmountable. Yet God says we will tread on them; they will not tread on us.

2. Young lion problems

The *young lions* are less obvious, smaller issues that can grow into full-scale problems if we don't handle them. These young lion problems come to harass and destroy us gradually like little foxes! Subtle negative thoughts that we won't be able to pay our bills or that our mate no longer loves us or that we are no longer in love with our mate are good examples of this category. Those little foxes will grow into big ones if they are not taken captive and destroyed (2 Cor. 10:4–5). Answer those little foxes with the Word of God. Small harassments, distractions, and irritations are young lions.

> Catch the foxes for us,
> The little foxes that are ruining the
> vineyards,
> While our vineyards are in blossom.
>
> —Song of Solomon 2:15

When our grandson Avery was four years old, he was living in Montana. His mother and daddy had taught him to take authority over sickness by saying

"By the stripes of Jesus I am healed." Then, instead of running to his mommy every time he got hurt, you could hear him say, "Devil, you can't hurt me—by Jesus' stripes I am healed." Or sometimes you could hear him say, "Pain, leave, in Jesus' name"—and then he would usually go right on playing. It is sometimes hard to believe that someone that young knew to do that, but it is because his parents taught him at an early age that he had authority and rights over sickness and accidents. So, even with things as small as it would take a Band-Aid to cover, Avery understood authority—that he could do this for himself and handle his own *young lion* problems.

Avery on left with his mom and dad, Peyton and Hunter

3. Cobra problems

God names *cobra* problems next. These are the problems that seem to sneak up on us like a *snake in the grass* throughout our day. They are what we might call an *undercover* attack that brings sudden death—a deceptive scheme keeping us blinded until it devours us. Thank the Lord we have authority to tread over such things so these surprise attacks will not overpower us.

One mother, Kim Hull, tells in her own words how God protected her and her children from one of these *undercover cobra attacks.*

> Our children attend a wonderful Christian school, and they have chapel every Monday morning with guest speakers coming to speak to the students about different topics to encourage them in their walk with Christ. One such Monday morning my son was singing and helping to lead worship prior to the speaker coming forward to share. I came to the chapel time to watch the praise team sing and was able to hear Angelia Schum speak to the students. We had never met, but I knew her by sight. After she spoke and during the quiet time, she turned around and asked my name. I affirmed that I was who she was inquiring about, and she started telling me about a dream she had in which my children and I were in a car wreck, and in the dream I was killed. She was very kind about it and didn't alarm me, but she explained that she believed sometimes dreams were

Dr. Hull and his family

prophetic so the situation could be handled, and she felt she needed to share the dream with me. After we talked awhile, she took authority and prayed some of the scriptures of Psalm 91 over me and also prayed that any assignment of Satan be broken over me and my family. I thanked her, and, at peace, I left and continued on with my busy life.

The next fall, the Sunday before school was to start, I had dropped a friend's daughter off after our evening church service. I came to a stoplight near her home and stopped, and then as the light turned green, I proceeded through the intersection. A drunk driver going sixty-five miles an hour down one of the main streets in our small town hit the front corner of the passenger side of our car. My car was completely spun around in the middle of the intersection on two tires before it came to rest and started smoking. I quickly urged all the children to get out of the car and head to the grass on the side of the road. My car was demolished, and the air bag on the driver's side of the other car deployed. One of the young men in our car slammed his elbow on the window, and it was sore, but other than that we walked away from a wreck that

> should have been devastating. We later discovered the friend who had bumped his elbow had a small fracture, which had to be cast, but that was the only injury. I believe with all my heart that if Angie had not shared her dream and prayed for the members of my family, that wreck's outcome would have been totally different. Our vehicle had been T-boned and pushed up on two wheels. We were spun around, landing the vehicle on another road, and the right side where the children were was crushed—and yet we walked out! When we went to see the car at the wrecking yard, it was shocking that everyone could have survived after the right side was demolished. I praise God for His provision and promise in Psalm 91 that He will take care of us.[1]

The *cobra* is a picture of when Satan sneaks up on you and tries to hurt you when you least expect it. It can be as deadly as a physical attack such as a car wreck or as simple as someone who tells lies about you behind your back. It is Satan who is using that person's mouth to try to hurt you and cause you to give up. We definitely need God's protection from *cobra* attacks.

4. Dragon problems

We might have guessed the lion and cobra analogies, but what are the *dragon* problems? I looked up the Hebrew word in *Strong's Concordance*, and it listed *sea monster*. First of all, there is no such thing as a dragon or a sea monster. Dragons are a figment of one's imagination. But have you ever experienced fears that were a figment of your imagination? Sure, you have. We all have!

For example, I know many people who are afraid of the dark! That's a *dragon* fear because the dark can't hurt anyone. It is the fear that will hurt you, much more than the thing you're afraid of. That is why God tells you *not to be afraid*. Imaginary fears can make you act very strangely. One child who was afraid of the dark would crawl into the corner of the room and cover herself with an umbrella.

Dragon problems represent our unfounded fears—phantom or mirage fears. That sounds harmless enough, but are you aware that phantom fears can be as deadly as reality fears if we believe them?

Some people's *dragon* fears are as real to them as another person's *lion* problems. That is why it is important to define your fears. So many people spend all of their lives running from something that is not even chasing them. Many people allow a *lion* problem they have already faced to become a *phantom* problem they battle the rest of their lives.

> The wicked flee when no one is pursuing.
> —Proverbs 28:1

This verse is a good definition of phantom fears. We have had a great many people share testimonies of God's deliverance from things like fear of the unknown, fear of facing the future alone, fear of loss, fear of death, tormenting suspicions, claustrophobia, and so forth.

Dragon fear is a very valid form of spiritual attack—especially for soldiers who have been subjected to extended periods of intense battle. When my daughter and her husband were first married, they lived in an apartment that was managed by a Vietnam veteran. Angelia came up behind him one day to bring their rent check, and he went into "attack mode." Afterward he apologized profusely, but his body was still living in a past time zone. He was out of danger, but he was still dwelling there. Others experience mental gymnastics and restless nights—rehearsing all the things that can go wrong in each situation. Dragon fears keep one living in the past or the future rather than experiencing life in the present. Fantasy fears can cause us to do a lot of unnecessary running in life, so authority over *dragons* is not a mental game.

All four categories

The good news, however, is that God says we will tread on *all* of the powers of the enemy—no matter how loud and bold, sneaky and deceptive, or imaginary those powers might be. God has given us authority over all of them! No longer are we to put up with the paralyzing fears that at one time gripped our hearts and left us powerless at the sight of the evil that was striking all around us. God has given us His *power of attorney*, and these problems now have to submit to the authority of His name. I like that word *tread*. I think of a tank crossing a brushy plain. Where the tank treads go, everything is crushed and left flat on the ground. It is a great picture of our authority over these spiritual enemies as well, treading like a tank and crushing all that is evil in our path. That is a strong description of our authority in walking over the lion, young lion, cobra, and dragon.

There are legitimate fears, and there are torments that the devil uses to plague our mind. Either way the fear has to be faced. Some people are afraid of the sound of thunder (dragon). Some people are afraid of sickness and injury (cobra). Some people are afraid after a bad dream (young lion). Some parents fear that their child will be killed in a car wreck. Some children go to bed every night afraid that their parent will be killed because, perhaps, the parent serves as a cop or soldier (roaring lion). In this fallen world we have legitimate times of crisis. But whether the danger is real or imaginary, we have been given a clear promise of authority in the form of the word *tread.*

> Behold, I [Jesus] have given you authority to tread on serpents and scorpions, and over all the power of the enemy, and nothing will injure you.
>
> —LUKE 10:19

There are promises that we can do this without being harmed. Most Christians, however, either do not know them or fail to use them. How often do we believe the Word enough to act on it? But the good news is that God says we will tread on *all* of the powers of the enemy—no matter how loud and bold, sneaky and deceptive, or imaginary those powers might be. God has given us authority over all of them! Kim's story was a prime example of how preventive prayer helped her tread over the attack that came to end the lives of her and her children.

Since the enemy comes both suddenly, without warning, and boldly defying us, we need to take authority over his tactics before they have a chance to pounce and overcome us.

Chapter

BECAUSE I LOVE HIM

Because he has loved Me, therefore I will…

—Psalm 91:14

In verses 14 through 16 God Himself starts talking to us directly, and He offers seven more promises to anyone who truly loves Him. Ask yourself, "Do I really love the Lord?" Be honest! God already knows the answer anyway.

A commitment to love involves choice. God has set His love on us in the same way this passage challenges us to set our love on Him. When we do, the promises come into effect. Love is what binds man to God, and God will be faithful to His beloved.

You may have watched in horror as your young child picked up a newly birthed kitten by the throat and carried it all over the yard. You may have wondered how the kitten ever survived.

In our family it was an old, red hen that endured the distress dished out by our very enthusiastic children. "Ole Red" would allow herself to be picked up while in the process of laying her egg and would deposit it right in Angie's eager little hands. The children had some merit to what they advertised as *the freshest eggs in town*—a few times the egg never hit the nest. Nesting season had its own special fascination for the children as they watched Ole Red try to hatch out more eggs than she could sit on. The kids would number the eggs in pencil to ensure each egg was properly rotated and kept warm—even rotating eggs between different chickens. They would wait out the twenty-one days and then, with contagious delight, call me out to see the nest swarming with little ones. That old hen had a brood of chicks that was hatched out of eggs from every hen in the henhouse.

Observing a setting hen this close had its own rare charm as one could witness the *protection* she gave those chicks in a way most people never have the chance to observe. I remember her feathers as she fanned them out. I remember the smell of the fresh straw the kids kept in the nest. I remember that I could see through the soft, downy underside and watch the rhythmic beating of her heart. Those chicks had an almost enviable position—something all the books on *the theology of protection* could never explain in mere words. This was the unforgettable picture of a real-life understanding of what it means to be *under the wings*. Those were some happy chicks! *True protection* has everything to do with *closeness*.

One reason we were created is for fellowship with the Lord. When David was just a shepherd boy, he would be out in the field at night watching over his sheep—playing his harp and singing love songs to the Lord. And do you remember what God said about David. God called him "a man after My own heart." There is nothing that God wants from you as much as He wants you to spend time talking to Him, listening to Him, and having fellowship with Him. The more time you spend with God, the more you will learn to trust Him and know that His Word is true. David learned to trust God, and that is why he was not afraid to fight the lion and the bear—and later the giant. God had become his best friend, and he knew that *God would never leave or forsake him*.

During one of the floods that we had in our town several years ago, Bill had a flock of goats on some land by the bayou. As the bayou water began to rise and overflow its banks, some men saw Bill's goats being overtaken by the flood, so they hoisted them up into the loft of a barn to keep them from drowning. By the next morning the water was like a rushing river—a mile wide—washing away uprooted trees and everything else in its path. Bill had, by this time, been told about his goats, so in spite of the road blocks and the rapids that were gushing by, he set out in an old tin-bottom boat across those swift floodwaters to rescue his little flock of goats. He knew that in another few hours they would die from thirst and suffocation.

Little Willie, his most precious goat of the entire herd because of being bottle-fed, was the first voice that Bill heard when he got close to the barn. And sure enough, when he was able to force the loft door open, while standing in his boat as it was being tossed about in the rushing waters, Little Willie was the first one to jump into his arms. Then, boatload by boatload, carrying just a few at a time, Bill was able to get every one of those goats down out of the loft and rowed to safety.

A television camera crew from Abilene was filming the flood, but when they saw the little goat boy risking his life to rescue his goats, that was the news story of the day—making the news at six o'clock and then again at ten. The love Bill had for those goats to risk his life to take them to safety is a picture of God's love for His children.

Knowing that God loves us is the glue that holds all of these promises together. Some people acknowledge that there is a God; others *know* Him. Neither maturity nor education nor family heritage... nor even a lifetime as a nominal Christian can make a person *know* Him. Only an encounter with the Lord and time spent with Him will cause one to lay hold of the promises in Psalm 91.

We need to ask ourselves, "Do I really love Him?" Jesus even asked this of Peter, a close disciple (John 21:15). Can you imagine how Peter must have felt when Jesus asked three times, "Peter, do you love Me?" Can you imagine your love being questioned? Even so, we need to question ourselves, because these promises are made only to those who have genuinely set their love on Him. Take special note of the fact that these seven promises in verses 14–16 are *reserved* for those who return His love.

Do you love Him? If you do, these promises are for you!

Chapter

GOD IS MY DELIVERER

Because he has loved Me, therefore I will deliver him.

—PSALM 91:14

A PROMISE OF DELIVERANCE IS the first of the seven promises made to the one who loves God. Make it personal! For instance, I quote it like this: "Because I love You, Lord, I thank You for Your promise to deliver me."

When I was young, I personally needed deliverance. I almost destroyed my marriage, my family, and my reputation because I was tormented with fear. One incident opened the door. I can remember the very instant my happy life changed into a nightmare that lasted eight years. And one verse walked me out of this living mental hell: "Whoever calls on the name of the Lord will be delivered" (Joel 2:32)! There are times when our children will desperately need God's promise of deliverance. The Word worked for me, it worked for my children, and it will work for you.

There are also other types of deliverances. There is the internal and the external. Ask yourself, "From what is He going to deliver me?" Remember the external deliverances discussed in previous chapters. God will deliver us from *all* of the following:

- Lion problems
- Young lion problems
- Cobra problems
- Dragon problems
- Terror by night—evils that come through man: war, terror, violence
- Arrows that fly by day—enemy assignments sent to wound
- Pestilence—plagues, deadly diseases, fatal epidemics
- Destruction—evils and natural disasters over which man has no control

In other words, God wants to deliver us from every evil known to mankind. That protection does not stop just because we or one of our children might be on foreign soil, alone on a dangerous mission, or in the midst of a fierce battle.

Deliverance is all encompassing. It happens within (internal) and without (external); in fact, it surrounds us.

> You are my hiding place; You preserve me
> from trouble;
> You surround me with songs of
> deliverance.
>
> —Psalm 32:7

Cordell had jumped into the van beside his father and watched as Barry pushed a broken Volkswagen into position for repairs and secured it with bricks under each tire. With that task finished, Cordell was headed down the hill toward home when he heard an odd sound, like the groaning and scraping of metal. Then he heard wheels spinning. Glancing over his shoulder, he saw the Volkswagen barreling down the hill after him. He didn't even have time to scream before the front tire, followed by the back tire, rolled over his neck, across his chest and down his abdomen. Debra flew out of the house when she heard Barry scream that the car had popped out of gear and run over Cordell! Barry checked his son and found the tire tracks on his neck and chest. A deep red mark marred his abdomen. His back bled from burrs and stickers embedded there. Nothing but a miracle could have saved him, and God's Psalm 91 protection did just that.

That night after Cordell was taken care of, Debra dove into the Bible with the ferocity of a lioness protecting her cub. She had searched the Scriptures for promises of protection and had learned the power of praying God's Word. She realized just how powerful Word-based prayers and God's Psalm 91 covenant could be. It was nothing short of the miraculous power of God's promises that had saved Cordell that night. It was from her studies that she learned about the protective power that resides in the blood of Jesus. If a lamb's blood under the old covenant could protect both people and animals from death, how much more the blood of Jesus!

Using her faith to apply it, Debra began praying the protective power of Jesus' blood over Cordell and the rest of her family every day. She found out later that everything she was learning from the Word was preparing her for some battles to come. When Cordell was nine, he took a bucket and went outside to feed the chickens. When he finished, he shut the door to the hen house but the latch didn't catch, so instantly

Cordell Sheffield

twenty-seven loose chickens squawked and flapped in the yard.

While Cordell was trying to shoo them back into the coop, a Brahma cow became riled at the squawking chickens and charged him. He sprinted for his life, but instead of outrunning the cow, he fell into the water tank and came up soaking wet, his blond hair plastered to his head and his jeans so heavy with water they slid low on his hips and threatened to collapse around his ankles. His mom was able to help him get the Brahma cow into another pasture, and they began chasing the chickens toward the coop. One of them, however, scurried for cover under an old Monte Carlo—a restoration project that had never gotten off the ground.

Using a rake, Cordell tried to shove the chicken out from under the car. Cordell heard the word *snake* echo inside of him like an announcement on a loud speaker, but he passed it off, thinking it was probably just his imagination. Suddenly he let out a yelp and grabbed his leg just above the knee. He yelled again, this time falling backward onto the hot, wired fence. Draped in wet clothes, he couldn't get off before the electrical current burned through him like lightning.

He told his mom that something had bitten him, but Debra couldn't find any mark on his leg, so they went back to herding the chickens and worked for another thirty minutes before Cordell stopped and said, "Mom, my leg is really burning." She still couldn't see anything, but panic hit when Cordell told her that his leg was beginning to feel numb. Calling 911 got an ambulance there within minutes, and one of the paramedics took a look at Cordell's leg and pointed out two snakebites.

Debra grabbed her Bible and cell phone before speeding away in the ambulance. One of the paramedics called the nearest hospital. "We've got a snake-bit kid. Do you have any antivenin for children?" All they had was adult antivenin. Hospital after hospital was called, and they found the antivenin they needed was only available at Children's Hospital in Oklahoma City. By this time Cordell had broken out in a cold sweat and was feeling dizzy. The paramedic pricked Cordell with needles and found he was numb to his waist. Then her son whispered to her that he didn't know if he would make it to Oklahoma City. Fear gripped Debra so hard she struggled to catch her breath. With hands shaking, she called her friends and church members for prayer. "Cordell's been double snake bit! He needs prayer!"

As she snapped her cell phone shut, one of the paramedics said, "You have the answer in your lap. Why don't you open it?"

Still shaking, Debra looked down and saw her Bible. Her phone rang, and one of her friends said, "The Lord gave me Acts 28:3 and 5 where Paul was bitten by a snake. According to the Bible he shook it off and never got sick. The Lord told me that the same thing will happen to Cordell."

Debra opened her Bible to Psalm 91 and began reading it as a prayer over her son. When she reached verse 13, she almost shouted with joy. "You will tread upon the lion and the cobra, the young lion and the serpent you will trample down." Faith welled up in her, fear fled, and she took authority over the snakebite.

An hour and a half after the first snakebite, the ambulance flew into Children's Hospital. After examining Cordell, the head of the children's department pulled Debra aside. "All I can say is that your son is a very lucky boy. It must have been a dry strike. That means it bit something else before it bit Cordell." Since a lot of people have died from a dry strike, the doctor gave him antivenin anyway.

There was never even any swelling, and by the time he arrived at the hospital, the numbness was gone. Today Cordell Sheffield is twelve years old, happy, healthy, and still living under the protection of the blood of Jesus. Thank God, Cordell's parents know the power of Psalm 91 and live under its protection.

If there is ever a group of people who need Psalm 91 promises, it is those who have "accident-prone" children in their family, but God's Word offers His promise to deliver if we will simply love Him and believe Him for it.

Chapter

I AM SEATED on HIGH

Because he has loved Me . . . I will set him securely on high, because he has known My name.

—Psalm 91:14

To be set securely *on high with God in heavenly places* is the second promise to those who love the Lord and know Him by name. He has "raised us up with Him [Jesus], and seated us with Him in the heavenly places in Christ Jesus" (Eph. 2:6).

What does it mean to be seated with Christ in

heavenly places? It is interesting that God pulls us up to where He is! Things look better from higher up. Our vantage point is much improved, seated with Him on high. So if He is seated above everything on earth—when we walk in His ways and do His will, we are above everything too. All the evil in this world is under our feet.

Think what it is like to be seated on high in heavenly places. When we realize where we are sitting spiritually, it gives us a whole new outlook. When you were little, did you ever go to a parade and were not able to see any of the floats because of all the people in front of you? That happened to me once, and I remember my father picking me up and putting me on his shoulders. It was wonderful because from that high up, I was able to see the whole parade—and not just the part that was passing right in front of me. I could also look all the way down the street and see what had already passed and what was coming. That's what God does for us. We can see things the way God sees them—from His heavenly perspective.

It is so important to realize that there is a name you call on that will save you. It can set you securely on high. Many times we lose spiritual battles with our mouths, and we open ourselves up for assaults. An environment of negative complaining opens the door to have more happen to us to complain about, yet calling on God for help renders aid. I challenge you to meditate on God's promise: "I will set him securely on high, because he has known My name" (Ps. 91:14). These are not just empty words.

What all does verse 14 mean when it says we have known His name? What all is there to know about God's name? When God wanted to show the people something important about Himself or about His promises in the Old Testament, He would make it known by telling the people another one of His names. For example, when He wanted Abraham to know that He would provide everything that Abraham would ever need, God told Abraham that His name was *Jehovah-Jireh*, which means "I am the Lord who provides." God wanted the Israelites to know that He was their healer, so He told them that His name was *Jehovah-Rapha*, which means, "I am the Lord who heals." There are many names of God, and each of those names tells us something else that God will do for us—that is how each name of God tells us a great deal about Him.

Our granddaughter Jolena experienced firsthand seeing her son set on high above death and disaster. She tells that story in her own words:

> Our family snuggled up under a blanket to watch the fireworks show on July 4, 2011, then started down the hill to our car to head home. It was very dark, and the traffic was crazy with so many families getting into

cars and then pulling out onto the highway. I was glad there were so many traffic workers manning the crowd. My husband, Heath, and our two boys were crossing the highway, and I was just a few feet away with my hands full of camera bags and my purse, and holding onto six-year-old Peyton. Heath also had his hands full with the two boys, pulling the wagon with all of our things, and managing our dogs on leashes. He was watching for a chance to cross the street, and I heard him holler, "GO" to the boys! The coast was clear, so Peyton and I also started across the road, when Avery, our oldest, ran ahead!

To everyone's surprise, this car came speeding out of the dark, and I watched helplessly as it plowed right into Avery. Shocked by seeing my son struck by a car, I dropped Peyton's hand, threw all my things in the middle of the highway, and began running toward Avery just as I saw him fly up in the air and come down on his head on the hood and windshield of the car, then roll off onto the ground, landing on his feet. Almost

Avery is the one in the middle

in one motion he looked back at me and said, "I'm OK, Mom! I'm OK!" I grabbed him and started screaming out to Jesus. I wish I could tell you that I was calm, cool, and collected, but I was shouting at the top of my lungs, "We have Psalm 91 protection!" I'm sure they could have heard me a block away, but as I looked at the car and saw the damage, I got even louder. I guess that was coming out of me because there's not a morning when I don't pray Psalm 91 over the children.

The front metal bumper on the car that hit Avery was bent, the hood had a big dent, the windshield was cracked all the way across, and in a separate spot there was a big spider-web crack!

Instantly Heath was there, and with his flashlight, he was checking Avery over from head to foot. (I can always count on him to be calm.) A woman came and stood with Hunter and Peyton. The lady who was driving the car had gotten out and kept asking over and over if he was OK. I couldn't even respond to her. There was a defiant man in the car with her, and he and Heath got into an argument that was escalating until I shouted out to Heath to stop it! Later that night the police officer on the scene came to the hospital to check

> on Avery and told us that the lady who hit him and the man who was with her had been drinking, and she had been arrested for reckless driving and taken to jail.
>
> Emergency workers had checked Avery over carefully at the scene, then again at the emergency room. While we were waiting for the doctor to read the X-rays, Avery told me, "Mom, I already knew that God loved me and had a plan for my life, but now I really know He has something special for me to do!" The doctor said Avery was just fine. They could find nothing wrong—no injuries whatsoever. They sent us home, and we kept close watch, waking him and checking him. I kept looking for a bruise or a mark, but there was nothing! It was nothing short of supernatural to see the damage that boy did to the car, yet the car didn't do damage to our ninety-pound son!

This promise of being seated securely on high is for the one who loves God and truly knows Him by name. We need to ask ourselves this question: "Does the position God has raised me to cause me to see things more His way, or do I quickly forget all He has done for me?" My beliefs and actions should reflect that I am seated on high because He has loved me.

Chapter

GOD ANSWERS MY CALL

He will call upon Me, and I will answer him.

—Psalm 91:15

The third bonus promise from God is to *answer* those who truly love Him and call on His name. Think about what that verse is saying to you.

When I think of how God answers when we call, I think of the day when we came home and found that the car belonging to our teenagers had been stolen from the carport. We called a family meeting and asked God to return the car. He told us to choose to forgive the one who had taken it. That was hard at first, but since forgiveness is a choice, not a feeling, we made a sincere choice to forgive. Forgiving them didn't seem to help the situation. The sheriff's department told us that they didn't think we would ever see that car again since it had been gone for almost a week. It was hard to ignore that negative report, but we just kept believing that God would do a miracle. We knew that even if we never saw that car again, we would still love and trust God, but we didn't want the devil to win. And sure enough, after another week a miracle happened. A man turned himself in and said that he had stolen things all of his life, but this was *the first time he had ever felt guilty.*

The man told us that he had left the car on the parking lot of the rodeo grounds in a nearby town. Sure enough, when we drove up, there it was—exactly where he had said. *We called on God as a family, and, just as He promised, He answered.*

It is so important to teach our children about calling on God. So many people make their little ones rely on learning how to dial 911. They practice and practice with them to make sure they never forget, but so often they fail at teaching their children to call on heaven. How many times have we seen that earthly emergency help could not get there in time, but God's help is as near as the air we breathe? When children see by example how a family can call on God, it is the most natural thing in the world for them to do it for themselves, just as Bill, in the next example, found himself in a position where no one could get there fast enough to help him.

Jack and our son, Bill—not knowing there was an old underground gas well at the back of our property—were burning brush. As you can imagine, when the fire got over the gas well it literally exploded, sending fire in every direction and igniting a nearby tall, dry, grass field. Immediately the fire was completely out of control. With no water lines back there at the time, they were fighting to no avail. Even the barrel of water they had in the back of the pickup didn't make a dent in the flames.

Seeing that the fire was getting dangerously close to other fields that led right into the surrounding homes, Jack flew up to the house to call the fire department, sent me to meet them at the crossroads so they wouldn't get lost, and then dashed back—only to find that the fire was out. And Bill, looking like he had been working in the coal mines, was sitting on a tree stump trying to catch his breath. Jack said, "How on earth were you able to put out the fire? There was no way." When you think about the promise that when we call upon Him, He answers us, then Bill's next words to Jack—"I called on God"—said it all.

What tremendous testimonies there are declaring what God has done when we have called upon Him. This promise is so important for those surprise attacks in life!

Chapter

GOD RESCUES ME FROM TROUBLE

> I will be with him in trouble; I will rescue him...
>
> —Psalm 91:15

The fourth bonus promise—to *rescue from trouble* those who love the Lord—is found in the middle of verse 15. It is a well-known fact that human nature cries out to God when faced with trouble. Men in prison, soldiers in war, people in accidents—all seem to call out to God when they get in a crisis. Even atheists are known to call on *the God they don't acknowledge* when they are extremely afraid. A lot of criticism has been given to those kinds of "court of last resort" prayers. However, in defense of this kind of praying, we must remember when one is in pain, he usually runs to the one he loves the most and the one he trusts. The alternative is not calling out at all, so this verse acknowledges *calling out to God in trouble* is a good place for a person to start!

God answers our prayers and rescues us in so many different ways. I am so thankful He is creative and not hindered by our seemingly impossible situations. But we have to ask in faith and not confine Him to our limited resources. This verse lets us know how it works: If you love Me... I will be with you when you find yourself in trouble, and I will rescue you. But we have to trust Him to do it *His* way.

> When you pass through the waters, I will
> be with you;
> And through the rivers, they will not
> overflow you.
> When you walk through the fire, you will
> not be scorched,
> Nor will the flame burn you.
>
> —ISAIAH 43:2

Our son, Bill, once saw the *rescuing* power of God when he found himself in serious *trouble* after attempting to swim across a lake that was much wider than he calculated. With no strength left in his body, and having already gone under twice, Bill experienced all the sensations of drowning. But miraculously God not only provided a woman on the opposite previously deserted bank, but He also enabled her to throw a life ring (that just *happened* to be nearby) more than thirty yards, landing within inches of his almost lifeless body. Although some people might call happenings like these a coincidence, the negative situations that we encounter can become *God-incidences* when we trust His Word. That was certainly Bill's *day of trouble*, but I thank God He was with Bill and *rescued* him.

One of my favorite stories of God's miraculous rescue happened the year I wrote my first book. When God delivered Skylar, it was such an encouragement to our entire church and such a confirmation to me that I was called to share these miracles as an affirmation to His promises in Psalm 91. Skylar's mother, Audra Chasteen, gave this testimony in our church of how Psalm 91 saved her four-year-old child:

> About 7:30 in the evening on July 28, 2001, three of my sisters and I, along with our children, were visiting my parents. Skylar, my four-year-old, was riding bicycles with the older boys out in the pasture about a

half-mile from the house. I had just turned to warn my older son not to ride down the hill because of the steep incline, when I realized that Skylar had already started down. The next thing I knew the bicycle was out of control, and he had gone over the side of a cliff. When I got to him, he wasn't moving and he wasn't crying. He was tangled in the wheel of the bicycle, lying on his stomach, with his chin twisted past his shoulder and resting on his shoulder blade. It was a terrifying sight to see Skylar's head twisted backward. His left arm was back behind him with his wrist above his right shoulder. His eyes were half open, in a fixed position down and to the corner. He was blue and not breathing.

In spite of the obvious head and neck injury, I turned his head forward so that he could breathe. But when he still didn't start breathing, I turned his whole body straight, hoping that would help. When that didn't work, I became hysterical. My three sisters and I are nurses, one RN and three LVNs, but we couldn't seem to pull ourselves together to know what to do medically.

Skylar Chasteen

When my oldest sister, Cynthia, finally got to the scene of the accident, the first thing she did was to lay her hand on Skylar's head and start rebuking the enemy. She kept saying, "I rebuke you, Satan, in the name of Jesus—you get your hands off Skylar—you cannot have him!" Then she started pleading the blood of Jesus and quoting Psalm 91 over him. Hearing God's Word coming out of Cynthia's mouth pulled me back to my senses. I sent one of my sisters for her car, and we headed for the nearest hospital—which was about seventeen miles away.

On the way to the hospital we did some rescue breaths on Skylar, and he would breathe for a few minutes and then stop. Cynthia and I continued to speak Psalm 91 over Skylar and to command his body to line up with God's Word.

When we got to the hospital in Comanche, Texas, he started throwing up—another sign of a bad head injury. The X-rays showed an obvious break in the C-1 vertebra (the first vertebra under the head), and Skylar still wasn't responding. He, along with the X-rays, was immediately put on an air flight to Cook's Children's Hospital in Fort Worth, Texas.

Since I was still in my scrubs from working all day, they didn't realize at Cook's Children's Hospital that I was the mother, so they had me helping to draw the blood on Skylar. I was listening as the trauma nurse reported to the doctor when he came in—"He has a C-1 fracture, his eyes are deviated and down to the left, he stopped breathing..." and so forth. The doctor was shocked when he discovered I was the mother. I could never have been that peaceful without all the prayers. Finally they wheeled him in for more X-rays and a CAT scan to see if there was any bleeding in the brain cavity.

When the doctor finally came in, he had a very strange look on his face, and all he could say was, "He's going to be all right!" Then after consulting with the radiologist, they came in saying, "We don't know how to explain this, but we can find no head trauma (brain swelling or bleeding), and we cannot find a C-1 fracture." They had the Comanche hospital X-rays with the obvious break, but their X-rays showed no sign of a break.

There are no words to describe the joy, gratitude, and excitement we felt at that moment. All the nurses were pouring in to tell us how "lucky" we were, and all I

> could say was, "Luck had nothing to do with this. This was God!" I was not about to let Satan have one ounce of glory. I knew that it was a miracle and that it was God who had healed him. The doctor was just amazed. He said, "I don't know what to tell you. There was definitely a break on that other X-ray, but he is obviously OK now. I don't know how to explain it." He didn't have to explain it. I knew what had happened. God is so good!
>
> Since the day we left the hospital, Skylar has been a perfectly normal, healthy little boy with no problems and no side effects from the accident. He is truly a miracle! Truly we experienced the rescuing power of God that day.

You too can experience that same rescuing power of God. The promises of Psalm 91 are His love gift to those who love Him and believe and confess His Word.

Chapter

GOD HONORS ME

I will... honor him.

—Psalm 91:15

The fifth promise to those who love God is to be honored. Do you like to be honored? Of course you do! I can remember when the teacher called my name while I was in grade school and complimented my work on a paper I'd turned in. That thrilled me. I was honored.

Most schools have an awards day when different students are given special awards. When your name is called out and an award is handed to you in front of all the other students, it is an honor. Cullen was thrilled when he received special football awards for his participation in the six-man football team at the Christian academy where he is a junior. He was awarded "First Team All-State Tight End in all of Texas and Second Team All-State Defensive End in Texas" as a sophomore. Those were special awards that honored him.

When my mother was a teenager, the honor she thought she was receiving from her junior high school physical education teacher turned out to fit the situation quite well, and it was an experience she never forgot.

Mother (Arma Lee) and her close friend, Dorothy Nell, were in junior high school. Feeling quite grown up and important, one day they decided to play hooky. Mother's house was located directly behind a large funeral home and faced the back entrance that lead into a massive storage area where all the caskets were kept. This particular day Arma Lee and her friend decided it would be fun to slip into that huge storage room and look at the caskets. However, once inside, just walking through and looking didn't satisfy their curiosity, so they opened one of the caskets and were quite impressed with the beautiful satin lining.

By this time their inquisitiveness had gotten the best of them, and they decided they needed to climb inside one of the caskets and experience what that felt like. Caught up in the amusement, they finally took turns crawling in a casket and letting the other one shut the lid and preach their funeral service. By the time they pulled themselves away from their fun, they had somehow missed a whole day of school. Feeling a little guilty that afternoon, Mother confessed to my grandmother what she had done. My sweet grandmother, who had so much goodness in her soul, couldn't fathom that this was any more than a tall tale, and she simply said, "Now, sis, you know that didn't happen." Mother felt relieved since she had gotten the parental resolution her soul needed after confessing her misdeeds.

Walking into their PE class the next day, the teacher very graciously told Mother and her friend that the class had learned a new exercise the previous day, and she wanted them to try it once before they continued exercise plans for that day. The girls were so excited to find that the teacher was not going to punish their unexcused absence that they sprang for the chance to learn the new routine. She had them get down on all fours next to the wall and then see which one of them could bring one foot and leg up the highest on the wall. Both girls, being quite competitive, almost split themselves in half trying to top the other. When they had both stretched their leg as high as they possibly could, the teacher said, "Arma Lee, your toes are higher. I believe you won. Now say, 'Bow-wow!'" With that she and the rest of the class roared with laughter. (A teacher probably could not get by with that today, but it accomplished its purpose back then.) The "honor" that Arma Lee and Dorothy Nell got that day definitely fit their crime.

That was an honor in reverse. None of us would like that kind of recognition.

We all like to get a real honor, but have you ever thought about what it means to be honored by the God of the universe? He honors us by calling us His sons and daughters. He honors us by answering when we take His Word seriously and call out to Him in faith. He honors us by recognizing us individually and by preparing a place for us to be with Him eternally. *Giving us honor* is one of the seven unique, bonus promises God made to us in Psalm 91.

Chapter

GOD SATISFIES ME WITH LONG LIFE

With a long life I will satisfy him.
—Psalm 91:16

"Peggy Joyce, I want to buy several hundred of your books to give away at my one hundredth birthday party!" That was a phone call I received a few years back when a lady from Minnesota called me one Saturday morning. She was so excited about giving these as gifts to each of her friends who came to her party. Most people would be thinking about the big party and all the gifts they would be getting—especially on their hundredth birthday—but this lady was thinking about what she could do for everyone else. That is a good example of someone who has lived a long, satisfied life. And one can't get that kind of satisfaction any other way, except by walking closely to Jesus.

The sixth promise is that God will give the one who loves Him a long, full life. God does not want us to just have a lot of birthdays. Some people have had a great many birthdays, but they were never happy. God says He will give you many birthdays, and as those birthdays roll around, you will be satisfied and feel complete.

Everyone has an empty place inside of his heart, and nothing will fill that emptiness except Jesus. People down through the ages have tried to fill it with different things, but the things of this world will not bring lasting satisfaction. Only after you decide to follow fully after God and give Him your whole heart will He fill your life to overflowing. Then you will experience a joy that you don't even have words to describe.

> Who [God] satisfies your years with good things.
>
> —Psalm 103:5

So many of our military men fear they will never see long life because of the dangerous lives they have to lead. But God's promises can work even in the midst of the most treacherous circumstances. Jacob Weise is living proof of that. Jacob was an infantry machine-gunner and a corporal in Gulf Company, Second Battalion, First Marines. He tells of his experience with Psalm 91 during his two deployments in the Iraqi war:

> In my first deployment we inserted into Iraq the first day of the war and assaulted and secured the city of An Nasiriyah in a night operation as we drove into the heart of the area along with other Marine and Army units. Our second deployment began on February 28, 2004, and involved seven months of operations in and around the city of Al Fallujah. Fallujah, unlike An Nasiriyah, was considered entirely hostile, and we had to deal with the daily changing rules of engagement; the brutal, adaptive, and unpredictable enemy; and the extremely untrustworthy, unreliable Iraqi forces. This made Fallujah a frustrating and dangerous place.
>
> During this time, however, I always felt protected. I was almost always at peace in my mind that the Lord was watching over me. This was largely due to the fact

that before I left for boot camp, I had taken hold of one thing—the Ninety-First Psalm and the power and promises contained in its verses, which protect us from every form of evil the enemy tries to bring against us. Right in the middle of this fight for our lives, my mind flashed back to that day when I first heard Peggy Joyce give the most complete breakdown of Psalm 91 that I had ever heard. It was hard for me to imagine the power that was locked into that psalm, but that was when I decided to pray it every day over myself and over the guys with me. June 24, 2004, was a testimony to the power that covenant promise carries.

My company held what we called the clover-leaf on the eastern edge of Fallujah from June to September of 2004. This is a major highway intersection that links Ramadi, Fallujah, and Baghdad. On the morning of the twenty-fourth, when we arrived at the clover-leaf, the fire had intensified to an insane level. The buildings on the northern and western sides gave the insurgents perfect cover to lay intense, concentrated small arms and RPG fire on our positions. Even as our fire support began to come on scene, the insurgents didn't let up. The Cobras were the first to arrive and hadn't been there long before one of them was shot down by a Stinger missile. I had never been under that intense a barrage of fire before. I remember praying the whole time I was out there. Without stopping, I was praying in the Spirit and praying the Ninety-First Psalm over us. As the tanks and eventually the AC-130s and the F-18s began to level the buildings dangerously close to our forward fighting holes, the insurgent barrage began to let up and finally lulled after an approximate six to seven hours exchange of fire.

Miraculously we did not have one single KIA (killed in action). Sniper fire had resulted in two of our Marines, including our company commander, being shot in the head. In both cases, however, the bullets had not penetrated the bone. They left only a nasty gash where the bullet traveled under the skin along the skull and out the back. The physician called them flesh wounds. How many times would a direct shot in the head be called a "flesh wound"? And it didn't happen just once but twice in the same battle. That was nothing but miraculous.

The most important part of all is the fact that during all of that, as I rolled through the Ninety-First Psalm in my head, I never felt like anything ever came remotely close to me. In April I had a mortar round hit so close that it killed the Marine in front of me and wounded two others around us, but I didn't feel so much as shrapnel go by me. Despite weeks and weeks of off and on firefights, we didn't suffer a single KIA throughout the months of June, July, August, or September. I believe that is a direct result of the covering of prayer over me, and covering my company as well. Psalm 91 really is a powerful thing that will bring you through. He protects you not only physically but spiritually as well. Transitioning back to life in the States, being home with my wife, and working with the drastically different garrison, baseline Marine Corps has really been no problem for me. I credit that to the fact that God protected my mind and soul as well as my body.

I know that it is not easy to listen to someone talk about Iraq and give an opinion—especially when it comes from a civilian who hasn't been there, done, seen, or experienced what we have. The word in this book, however, is relevant and real. It is truth. I witnessed miracles from the hand of God simply by believing and standing on the Word of God in Psalm 91. Please take it to heart. It will save your life and the lives of others.

Jake's mother, Julie Weise, writes:

When my son Jacob (Jake) was born, little did I know that twenty-one years later he would be one of the first United States Marines to cross the border into Iraq. He has since served two tours in that land called Babylon in the Bible—the land where Abraham and Daniel and so many others lived.

Was it a fearful time for me as the mother of a Marine infantryman? I can say to you that I was never afraid for my son. People who were close to me offered comfort and tried to console me. They didn't understand that I really was OK. As much as I appreciated the love they showed me, my comfort came from God and His Word. Jesus said, "Peace I leave with you…not as the world gives do I give to you. Do not let your heart be troubled, nor let it be fearful" (John 14:27). God's peace is total peace. My husband, my daughter, Mary, and I have a strong belief in the promises of God. We know Jake and his wife, Jeanine, feel the same way. He went into battle with God's Word in his heart. He took his Bible and carried a copy of Psalm 91 in his pocket. Before he left, we laid hands on him and prayed for his safety, asking God to bring him home whole in body, mind and spirit. And He did just that.

During those uncertain days God comforted us in many ways. Circumstances in the natural looked uncertain, but when we watched the television and heard reports of the fighting, we took comfort in our faith and in the promises of Psalm 91. The news could make a person go crazy with worry if you didn't have the promises of Psalm 91. Many people were praying and standing with us. There were times when Satan tried to whisper in my ear—thoughts of fear and doubt—thoughts of death and loss. But I had read God's Word, and I knew His promises—promises not just for heaven, as wonderful as that will be, but also promises of protection and provision here on earth. *Faith is a choice*. When the temptations came, I would go to God's Word and say, "No, we have

Jake and his mother, Julie Weise

> prayed the blood of Jesus over Jake. He is safe. God's Word is true."
>
> Jake wrote about one ambush they experienced when six men were shot by snipers, but they all completely recovered. They were penned down and had little cover. He told us he prayed all that night and read Psalm 91 over and over, putting in his name and the name of his company. God was faithful. All of the men survived with no permanent wounds and no deaths.
>
> It made it easier to pray for my son because I knew he also had faith and we were in agreement, but even if your son is not a believer, you can keep your loved one covered with prayer and you can know that God hears you.

One of the most challenging things is when a parent has to allow his or her child into harm's way as a soldier or on a mission field in a dangerous location. These stories inspire us to trust those we love to God.

God wants us to claim the promise of long life, but He also wants us to use our long life living for Him. Ask yourself, "What *am* I going to do with my long life that will qualify me as having lived a satisfied life?"

Chapter

I BEHOLD HIS SALVATION

. . . and let him behold My salvation.
—Psalm 91:16, nas, 1977

Many people are surprised when they look up the word *saved* or *salvation* in the Bible. Do you know what it means? Most people think it just means a ticket to get into heaven. It means that, but it means so much more. The word *salvation* also means health, healing, deliverance, protection, and provision. That means you can live in *health*, but if you happen to get sick, then God can give you *healing*! It means that He will *deliver* you from evil things that are causing you chaos. He will *protect* you from harm, and He will *provide* everything you need to have a full life. A person who doesn't know God might think this is impossible, but that is just because he doesn't know the promises of our powerful God.

Jennifer McCullough wrote about her experience with Psalm 91:

> Before leaving for East Africa in 1999, I was being discipled by Angelia Schum, my college Bible study teacher. It was a crash course in everything you need to know before entering "the Bush"! I ran into Angie's friend Donna one night at church. She said, "You do know about Psalm 91, don't you?" When I said no, she said, "Angie must not love you very much if she hasn't told you about Psalm 91!" That got my attention!

Jennifer McCullough

> I began intently studying the chapter and memorized it before I left. I had no idea the power this passage has until January 15, 2000. I lived in a village in the bush with the Ankole tribe (cattle herders), working with orphans with AIDS and teaching at the village school. I often found myself praying Psalm 91 while

walking the circumference of the village. I had gone to the city the day before on the milk truck. That night I was lying in my hut and heard gunshots. I ran to a fellow missionary's hut and sat in a small room praying Psalm 91 over and over. The husband was out investigating, so it was just a twenty-four-year-old mother, her two-year-old child, and me.

In the meantime a group of rebels were raiding my village. Men were shot, a pregnant woman was beaten, villagers were robbed, and cattle were stolen. The villagers were laid out in a line on their stomachs with guns and machetes pointed to their heads, while they were being threatened not to say a word. The raid was well planned as they had been watching us for days from the bushes.

Here is the miracle! Village people know that white missionaries have more in their huts than Ugandans make in a lifetime. Yet the rebels never came to our hut—despite the fact that everyone else's hut was raided. After the fact the rebels admitted to the police that they had followed the milk truck through the bush the night before the raid. I had been on that truck sitting next to the driver, who was carrying two million shillings—the villagers' monthly income from the milk sales. They did not attack the truck en route because we had returned before dark that night. This was the first time we had ever returned before dark in the six months I had been riding the route.

The day after the attack it was very intense. I walked through the village, praying for villagers who had been robbed and beaten. They had looks of pure terror on their faces, knowing that the rebels were still hiding in the bush nearby. As I was talking to the villagers, no one could believe that I was not attacked. My interpreter, Segambe, said, "*It was as if your hut was not even there.*"

God is faithful! He has a perfect plan for your life. God is all knowing! He will give you weapons to fight the battles you face. God did not give Psalm 91 only to missionaries in the African bush. He gave it to everyone so that we can daily claim His promises to us as Christians. I find the words of Psalm 91 in my daily prayers from the first verse, "*He who dwells in the shelter of the Most High*...," to the last verse, "*With a long life I will satisfy him, and let him behold My salvation*" (NAS, 1977).

Jennifer's mother, Mamie McCullough, was a well-known motivational speaker with the late

Zig Ziglar; however, she shares here in a very personal way about the power of Psalm 91 and the importance of letting your child follow God, even into the darkest places where the gospel needs to be preached. Here is her story:

> One of the most difficult things for a mother to do is release a child to go to the mission field. Abraham had to let go of Isaac and in many ways a parent has to at some point release a child to follow God's will. That is why knowing the promises of Psalm 91 is so important for a mother's sanity. I should know.
>
> As a widowed mother of three children, Patti, Brian, and Jennifer, I had always felt God's hand on our family in a special way since Don's death in 1981. One of the commitments I made early in life was to serve the Lord, raise my children in church, and give them a good education both mentally and spiritually. This was a challenging duty, but I have felt God's hand in every event and stage of life. In 1999 I was faced with a hard decision—my baby, Jennifer, at twenty-two, immediately after receiving a degree in special education from Howard Payne University, called to tell me that she felt God was calling her to missions. This was not

completely surprising to me since we had been involved in feeding the homeless, visiting children's homes, and working with many missions. My children's grandparents had served on the mission field, and their father had been raised in South America. I also had a sister who was a missionary in Africa. This was all before Jennifer was born, and she was unaware of her heritage until after she felt God's call on her life. It was interesting to me that without knowing the family background, she felt God was calling her to Africa. My first response was, "I also talk to God, and He did not mention Africa." I realized, however, that when we raise our children to follow God's will, we do not have the right to dispute their calling. This was not an easy adjustment since she did not have any missions training and had no idea about the language. She was also not sponsored by any denomination or organization.

Jennifer and her mother, Mamie

She found an orphanage eight hours north of Kampala, East Africa, and she felt this was where God had called her to work to help educate the children and lead them to

Christ. The last Sunday before she was to leave Dallas and fly thirty hours from us, we were in church at Prestonwood Baptist, where she had attended since she was five. I began to weep during the song service, and she put her arm around me and said, "Mama, don't be upset about my leaving you all." I assured her that I was not upset, nor did I disagree with her decision, but she could not expect me not to cry. This was a mother's right.

We began reading the Ninety-First Psalm every day and claimed God's protection and safety. There was a peace in my heart that she was doing the will of God, but having my twenty-two-year-old daughter leave this country for an unknown territory was scary. She said that God had told her she would return to us unharmed. God is good, and that is exactly what He did. I will probably never know what all she experienced on that six-month mission, but through the years she has related many of her challenges. She was the only *white girl* for miles around, and she lived in a straw hut in the open air with no protection except her faith in the Lord. The adventure Jennifer shared in her testimony above was just one of the many experiences she encountered. That evening some of the guerrillas came out of the forest and actually killed the people. She saw some blood-curdling deaths all around her, but as she lay on the floor of the hut, praying, they finally left. After that horrendous occurrence God's protection over her was certainly obvious when someone asked the guerrillas the next day if they got the "white woman," and their reply was, "There was no white woman." No one could ever tell me that God does not build a wall of fire around His children. He was certainly faithful to cover Jennifer with His Psalm 91 covenant of protection.

Even while she was returning from Africa on a flight to Chicago and back to Dallas, she experienced another of His precious miracles. When she got off the plane in Chicago, exhausted after being on such a long flight, they told her that there was not a flight for her back to Dallas. But God had other plans. The attendant came back in a few moments, telling her to call us to meet her in Dallas at 9:00 p.m. They had a flight back to Dallas leaving in an hour. There has never been a better sight than seeing my youngest baby walk off that plane. The miracle, of course, was her safe return, but it was also miraculous that she was the only passenger on the plane

> from Chicago. She had been put on first class and was treated like royalty. We have never understood how that happened, but it did happen, and we were so grateful. It is such an honor to know that God has His hand on our life, and when we choose to serve Him, we can know that we have the best that life has to offer.

Jennifer came home from that trip, began seminary, married a young preacher, and is now serving as a children's pastor in Norman, Oklahoma. She has two small children, Sam, age six, and Sydney, age four; her husband, Scott, is teaching Bible and supporting her ministry.

Jennifer cared about the salvation of people she had never met, and God let her behold His salvation when she needed it the most. Thank goodness this promise doesn't wait to start in heaven.

Another great "behold your salvation" story is about Cali after a relative gave her *My Own Psalm 91 Book* when she was six years old. That night her dad read the book to her before she went to bed. Afterward they spent time talking about what each page meant. Then, as they read the prayer at the end of the book, Cali was told that was the prayer to pray when someone wants to give her heart to Jesus.

As her dad closed the book, she took it from his hands and turned to the prayer page. When he asked if she wanted to pray that prayer, she eagerly said, "Yes!" He explained what giving one's heart to Jesus meant and made sure she understood what she was doing. When she was still insistent that was what she wanted, he called his wife in and asked Cali to share with her why she wanted to give her heart to Jesus. Again, she said that she wanted Jesus to live in her heart, to have her sins forgiven, and live with Him forever.

Cali's mother read the prayer to her, and Cali repeated the words to God. Afterward these words were written in her book: "10/25/10, Cali prayed this prayer and asked Jesus in her heart. Today is her new birthday! Today she beheld the salvation of the Lord." The family was so excited they wrote a thank-you, saying, "Thank you for such a wonderful book that has brought our family closer together for eternity."

This *Psalm 91 for Mothers* book is filled with testimonies of people who have beheld their salvation. They have beheld their healings, they have beheld their deliverance from evil, they have beheld the protection of the Lord, and they have beheld His wonderful provision. You too can behold the salvation of the Lord in all areas of your life. I encourage you to read Psalm 91 every day as a prayer back to God. His faithfulness to these covenant promises truly is a shield, just as He promises in Psalm 91:4.

SUMMARY

NOTHING IN THIS WORLD is more reliable than God's promises—when we believe them, refuse to waver, and make His Word *our final authority* for every area of life.

There is, however, a uniqueness about this psalm. Promises of protection can be found throughout the Bible, but Psalm 91 is the only place in the Word where all of the protection promises are brought together in one collection—forming a covenant written through the Holy Spirit. How powerful that is!

I believe Psalm 91 is a covenant—a spiritual contract that God has made available to His children. It is desperately needed in these difficult days. There are some who sincerely ask, "How do you know you can take a *song* from the Psalms and base your life on it?" Jesus answered that question. The value of the psalms was emphasized when He cited them as a source of truth that must be fulfilled:

> Now He said to them, "These are My words which I spoke to you while I was still with you, that all things which are written about Me in the Law of Moses

> and the Prophets *and the Psalms* must be fulfilled."
>
> —LUKE 24:44, EMPHASIS ADDED

When Jesus specifically equates the Psalms to the Law of Moses and the Prophets, we see that it is historically relevant, prophetically sound, and totally applicable and reliable.

At a time when there are so many uncertainties facing us, it is more than comforting to realize that God not only knows ahead of time what we will be facing but also makes absolute provision for us.

Someone once pointed out, "It is interesting that the world must have gotten its distress 911 number from God's answer to our distress call—Psalm 91:1."

It seems only a dream now to think back to the time when my mind was reeling in fears and doubts. Little did I know when I asked God that pertinent question—"Is there any way for a Christian to escape all the evils that are coming on this world?"—He was going to give me a dream that would not only change my life but also change the lives of thousands of others who would hear and believe.

WHAT MUST I DO to BE SAVED?

WE'VE TALKED ABOUT PHYSICAL protection. Now let's make sure you have eternal protection. The promises from God in this book are for God's children who love Him. If you have never given your life to Jesus and accepted Him as your Lord and Savior, there is no better time than right now.

> There is none righteous, not even one.
>
> —ROMANS 3:10

> For all have sinned and fall short of the glory of God.
>
> —ROMANS 3:23

> But God demonstrates His own love toward us, in that while we were yet sinners, Christ died for us.
>
> —ROMANS 5:8

> For God so loved the world [you], that He gave His only begotten Son, that whoever

> believes in Him shall not perish, but have eternal life.
>
> —JOHN 3:16

There is nothing we can do to earn our salvation or to make ourselves good enough to go to heaven. It is a free gift!

> For the wages of sin is death, but the *free* gift of God is eternal life in Christ Jesus.
>
> —ROMANS 6:23, EMPHASIS ADDED

There is also no other avenue through which we can reach heaven other than Jesus Christ—God's Son.

> And there is salvation in no one else; for there is no other name under heaven that has been given among men by which we must be saved.
>
> —ACTS 4:12

> Jesus said to him, "I am the way, and the truth, and the life; no one comes to the Father, but through Me."
>
> —JOHN 14:6

You must believe that Jesus is the Son of God, that He died on the cross for your sins, and that He rose again on the third day.

> ...who [Jesus] was declared the Son of God with power by the resurrection from the dead.
>
> —Romans 1:4

You may be thinking, "How do I accept Jesus and become His child?" God in His love has made it so easy.

> If you confess with your mouth Jesus as Lord, and believe in your heart that God raised Him from the dead, you will be saved.
>
> —Romans 10:9

> But as many as received Him, to them He gave the right to become children of God, even to those who believe in His name.
>
> —John 1:12

It is as simple as praying a prayer similar to this one—if you sincerely mean it in your heart:

Dear God:

I believe You gave Your Son, Jesus, to die for me. I believe He shed His blood to pay for my sins and that You raised Him from the dead so I can be Your child and live with You eternally in heaven. I am asking Jesus to come into my heart right now and save me. I confess Him as the Lord and Master of my life.

I thank You, dear Lord, for loving me enough to lay down Your life for me. Take my life now and use it for Your glory. I ask for all that You have promised for me.

In Jesus' name, amen.

PERSONAL PSALM 91 COVENANT

COPY AND ENLARGE THIS Psalm 91 covenant prayer to pray over yourself or your loved one—inserting his or her name in blanks.

__________ dwells in the shelter of the Most High and he/she abides in the shadow of the Almighty. __________ says to the Lord, "My refuge and my fortress, my God, in whom I trust!" For it is God who delivers __________ from the snare of the trapper and from the deadly pestilence [fatal, infectious disease]. God will cover __________ with His pinions, and under His wings __________ may seek refuge; God's faithfulness is a shield and bulwark.

__________ will not be afraid of the terror by night, or of the arrow that flies by day; of the pestilence that stalks in darkness, or of the destruction that lays waste at noon. A thousand may fall at __________'s side and ten thousand at his/her right hand, but it shall not approach __________.

__________ will only look on with __________'s eyes and see the recompense of the wicked. For __________ has made the Lord his/her refuge, even the Most High, __________'s dwelling place. No evil will befall __________, nor will any plague come near __________'s tent. For He will give His angels charge concerning __________ to guard __________ in all his/her ways. They will bear __________ up in their hands, lest __________ strike his/her foot against a stone. __________ will tread upon the lion and cobra, the young lion and the serpent he/she will trample down.

"Because __________ has loved Me [God said], therefore I will deliver him/her; I will set __________ securely on high, because __________ has known My name. __________ will call on Me, and I will answer __________. I will be with __________ in trouble; I will rescue __________ and honor __________. With a long life I will satisfy __________, and let him/her behold My salvation."

NOTES

Chapter 5
A Mighty Fortress Is My God

1. Peggy Joyce Ruth and Angelia Schum, *Psalm 91* (Lake Mary, FL: Charisma House, 2010), 121–122.

Chapter 6
I Will Not Fear the Terror

1. Adapted from Ruth and Schum, *Psalm 91*, 138–141.

Chapter 7
I Will Not Fear the Arrow

1. Adapted from Ruth and Schum, *Psalm 91*, 132–135.

Chapter 11
No Plague Comes Near My Family

1. Old English proverb.

Chapter 13
The Enemy Is Under My Feet

1. Ruth and Schum, *Psalm 91*, 145–146.

ABOUT THE AUTHORS

PROMINENT AUTHOR AND SPEAKER Peggy Joyce Ruth has helped thousands of people to develop a closer love walk with God. Her messages challenge individuals in all walks of life to delve deeper into understanding God's Word. She offers practical principles for applying Scriptures to day-to-day living. After thirty years of teaching a weekly adult Bible study and helping her husband pastor in Brownwood, Texas, she now devotes most of her time to speaking engagements, conferences (stateside and overseas), military events, and writing books. You will laugh at the humorous stories as you relate to real-life accounts of God's Word working in people's lives. Her messages are broadcast and streamed on radio and are available for free on her website www.peggyjoyceruth.org.

Peggy Joyce writes about her daughter Angie: "There is nothing more fun than being in ministry with your children. This year Angie and I spent weeks in Israel working on a Psalm 91 book in Hebrew interviewing some of Israel's finest heroes, commanders, generals, and Schindler List survivors. We heard incredible stories of their protection firsthand. Below, we are in a

Sukkot tent visiting with Ezra Yahkim, a man who fought for the liberation of Jerusalem in 1948 and again in 1967.

"Angie works in college ministry, overseas college mission outreaches, and manages two Christian FM radio stations. She speaks four times a week for a variety of audiences and is an entertaining speaker. Many times we share the platform at conferences and retreats. Angie speaks on subjects such as '8 Strategies for Evangelism,' 'Rattle of the Snake (the key to Preventative Prayer),' 'Delivered From the Power of Harm,' 'Adventures and Risks in the Life of a Christian,' 'One Word From God Can Change Your Life Forever,' and 'God Is the Defense of Your Life.' Both teenagers and adults will enjoy the high adrenaline in her book *God's Smuggler, Jr.*, as she tells about adventures in smuggling Bibles into China."

For speaking engagement information, please call (325) 646-6894 or (325) 646-0623. To connect to stream broadcast, go to www.christiannetcast.com/listen/player.asp?station=kpsm-fm or go to our website's homepage at www.peggyjoyceruth.org and push LISTEN NOW.